I0041629

THE PERFECT PARTNER

Simon McCrum

BENNION
KEARNY

Published in 2025 by Bennion Kearny Limited

Woodside, Oakamoor, ST10 3AE, UK

www.BennionKearny.com

ISBN: 978-1-915855-41-1

Simon McCrum has asserted his right under the Copyright, Designs and Patents Act, 1988 to be identified as the author of this book.

Copyright Simon McCrum 2025. All Rights Reserved.

No part of this publication may be reproduced, stored in a retrieval system, or transmitted in any form or by any means, electronic, mechanical, photocopying, recording or otherwise, without the prior permission of the publisher.

A CIP catalogue record for this book is available from the British Library.

This book is sold subject to the condition that it shall not, by way of trade or otherwise, be lent, re-sold, hired out or otherwise circulated without the publisher's prior consent in any form of binding or cover other than that in which it is published and without a similar condition including this condition being imposed on the subsequent purchaser.

Bennion Kearny Limited. 6 Woodside, Churnet View Road, Oakamoor, ST10 3AE, United Kingdom.

I dedicate this book to the mighty Thompsons –
Tuesday, Sean, Gracie, Harry, Georgie, and Mike

Books in this Series

The Perfect Lawyer
The Perfect Legal Business
The Perfect Partner

Contents

INTRODUCTION

When I wrote my first book, "The Perfect Legal Business" back in 2020, I thought that other books relating to law firm management and growth might follow. I even listed the next two to be published in that book – "The Perfect Lawyer" and "The Perfect Partner".

A strange thing happened, though, when I came to write my second book, "The Perfect Lawyer". I stopped in my tracks quite early on when writing that book as it became immediately apparent that it was impossible to write a book about what made a perfect lawyer without dovetailing it with the themes in my first book. Lawyers were a fundamental part of the perfect legal business that I had been looking at. What would it have said about those first themes if the perfect lawyer in my second book could perform in ways that did not embrace those pillars?

I realised there was a symbiosis between the law firm and the lawyers. You can't have the perfect law firm without perfect lawyers, and you can't have (or expect) to have perfect lawyers if you aren't a perfect legal business. They each feed into each other and drive each other.

The real import of this train of thought didn't hit me, though, until I came to write this, my third book. I had long had it in mind to look at the whole "law firm Partner" thing, but whereas I had thought that it would be a free-standing analysis of Partners' roles and the requirements of them, I now saw that they were, in fact, the vital third leg of the tripod. Partners can't be free-standing islands, ploughing their own furrow in their own way.

Such is the structure and the operation of law firms, the Partners in those firms are key to what a law firm does, how it does it, how long it does it for, and therefore to what it achieves.

Thus, I came to the strong and actually very exciting conclusion that my three books all fitted together. They are a Management tripod, or trilogy. Take one of the legs of the tripod away and the tripod falls over.

You are unlikely to have perfect lawyers throughout a firm if you don't have Perfect Partners, and you simply can't have perfect lawyers or Perfect Partners if the legal business itself is enabling or driving the wrong behaviours on the part of its junior and senior people.

The trilogy, with this book, is now complete. The solid tripod that is the route to sustainable, qualitative success for law firms is clear for all to see.

So, let's turn to Partners. You will see from this book that – even in this modern world where there are huge numbers of Partners in the legal sector, huge numbers of Partners in single firms, and various types of Partners, including employed Partners – none of these trends reduce the status or impact of Partners in the eyes of the people around them in the firm, and in the eyes of people outside a firm. A Partner is a Partner is a Partner.

Firms need to recognise this when they appoint Partners, as a partnership will be judged according to the behaviours of the worst Partner. Partners are – or ought to be – the driving force behind a law firm. Differences in status within a partnership (Salaried, Fixed Share, Equity) actually hold little importance in the areas and in the constituencies that count. All these Partners can have an incredibly good impact on a law firm, or an incredibly bad impact.

In this book, I hope that I can show that whilst a Partner does need to be valuable to a firm, there are various ways to assess a Partner's value to a legal business. I come to the conclusion that whilst it is easy to measure a Partner's "plus" factors, such as billing and Business Development contributions – and these are indeed the things that law firms usually do measure – the gains that a law firm can make from these factors is small compared to another contribution that law firm Partners can make. I also conclude that even if a Partner does make apparent "plus" contributions, they can make devastating "minus" contributions at the same time, both directly (in terms of the harm they can cause) but also indirectly and profoundly because they are preventing something magical from taking place.

I often say there's not much, if anything, that my readers don't already know about how to manage and run a sustainably-growing, profit-rich, and cash-rich legal business. Indeed, lawyers repeatedly tell me that there's nothing in my books that they didn't already know.

There must be something of value in my books, though, as I've sold thousands across over 50 countries.

What I'm also told by many lawyers, partners, and firms, however, are the following things:

- You pull it all together so well into one place

- You show that there's no point turning just one dial, as all the moving parts are connected

- All the dials need to be turned up at the same time for maximum effect

- Once I started reading your book, I couldn't put it down

Hopefully, I have achieved these same great things with this book, too. By all means, let me know.

Simon McCrum, 2025

CHAPTER 1

A STARTING POINT

The knock on the office door was followed by a creak as it opened slowly. The door opened, and the Partner stood at the threshold. Sat behind a large desk in the office was a junior lawyer, engrossed in their work.

"You know that big case I'm working on?" asked the Partner.

Everyone knew about the big case that the Partner was working on. It was generating huge fees, it was monopolising the Partner's time and attention, and it was also known to involve real hostility between the combatants. It was feared that methods, shall we say, that were outside the White Book (you can see how old I am) and outside the litigation, were possibly being used to advance one side's case or to undermine that of the other.

"Well", continued the Partner, "it's really beginning to trouble me. I believe that the underhand methods that we feared to be in play, are indeed in play, and that I am now personally being targeted in a menacing way."

"Crikey", replied the junior lawyer – the junior lawyer who was keen to "get on" in the firm. "What do you mean?"

"It's not just me, either; it's now affecting my family", added the Partner.

"Goodness", responded the junior lawyer. "What on Earth has happened?"

The Partner explained the reason for his visit. "When we got back to our house last night, after my wife and I had been out, we immediately sensed that something was wrong.

"And then we saw it. People had been in our house and had deliberately moved things around to let us know that they had been there. It was really sinister. Things that had been on my wife's bedside table had been neatly put in her bedside drawer. I know why they did it – they're trying to frighten us off, and I can tell you, it is having the desired effect".

"That is awful", replied the junior lawyer.

"I've given it some thought, and I want to make some changes to stop me being targeted like that", said the Partner.

"Too right", agreed the junior lawyer. "You can't let that carry on".

"What I want", said the Partner, "is that from now on, we are going to stop using my name and my reference on the correspondence in that case."

"I can see why", said the junior lawyer.

And then the Partner continued.

"And we want to start using yours."

CHAPTER 2

PARTNERS

Boom. Open-mouthed? We're on a journey, and that's the start.

It's a sobering exercise, but when I work with law firms and we are in a session where the junior lawyers are grouped around tables, I ask them to imagine that they are setting up a law firm partnership with the people they are sitting with.

This is how it goes:

- You're setting up a business with people that you think you know

- You're putting your livelihood, wealth, good name, and probably your house, on the line

- You could be very lucky, or over time, the others might not all contribute to the business in the way you think they should

- Any one of them could do something that costs you a lot of money, that dims the lights, or that even switches the lights off

Becoming a Partner in a partnership is throwing your lot in with others you have to trust and on whom you have to rely to do the right thing, every day, including when no one is looking. The dream is therefore that all of them act and behave like The Perfect Partner.

To explore what makes The Perfect Partner, I'd like to take you on a journey. The destination will bring greater clarity and hopefully improved understanding of what a law firm, and its stakeholders and participants, require of the Partners in that firm.

And a lot is required of them, believe me. For, whilst it may feel – as you come and go to work in a law firm – that everything is peaceful and that the oil tanker will carry on moving relentlessly forward (laden with smiles and profit and pay rises), let me tell you, it is anything but that positive and that simple.

If you get it right – that is, if you get an awful lot of things right, all the time – and you have a fair wind behind you, it can indeed be a great life, delivering lots of good things, including a lot of money.

But let me tell you that owning and running a law firm can, in reality, be more of a nightmare than a dream, and it is getting harder each year. Old ways no longer work. What got you here won't get you there.

The ship that is a law firm continually goes through storm fronts – many of them, and often simultaneously. Piloting the ship is a mammoth task. I take my hat off to every Managing Partner or CEO or Managing Director of a law firm. Most people have no idea what you go through when you are sat in the lonely top seat.

What could rock the boat? What do Partners need to be ready for? Crikey. Where do we start?

- Clients are not hell-bent on making us all rich – they have a long list of demands, and "we want our lawyers to be expensive and profitable" is not one of them

- Watch clients turn on you when they think you've lost them even a small amount of money

- Your competitors never seem to stop trying to do things better, for less

- The volume of cash that exits a law firm every month is seismic – and it needs replacing every month, or the lights soon go out

- At any particular moment, even very successful law firms often haven't got cash reserves or access to cash that will cover the next few pay days

- Firms' prices are under pressure, just as lawyers and teams are usually working inefficiently in revenue-generation terms

- Lawyers work all day for clients but typically only work half the day for the business. They want "full time" benefits and rewards, though

- Direct Costs (lawyer salaries) and Indirect Costs (better known as Overheads) are going up every year – and they all have to be paid without any delay, and in cash

- There can be a disconnect between income and expenditure (and, more particularly, between cash coming in and cash going out)

- Profit is constantly challenged, and cash all the more so. It's really hard to make a buck nowadays, and converting that into the only stuff that counts (cash) is another challenge altogether

- Mistakes on files can happen, but they really cause havoc when it comes to securing your Professional Indemnity Insurance renewal at an acceptable price, or at all

- There are risks everywhere

- Law firms are essentially "people" businesses. People generate issues – the more people, the more issues. Growth has visible and invisible costs

- Regulation gets harder and broader – and the penalties for non-compliance are rising hugely

- IT and "tech" never stand still. Constant change is expensive and disruptive. "Change on top of change" is widely complained of

- There are people out there who can rob you (and hold you to ransom or even shut you down) without ever entering your building

- Lawyers love interpreting rules – provided those rules don't apply to them. Compliance with even fair regulations designed to manage serious risk is often seen as optional, particularly by Partners

- Something that happens amongst your people in one part of the business can explode into a grave employment law issue

- Did I mention AI?

- Bad lawyers can cause repeated, long-lasting headaches

- Good lawyers are being poached all the time, and the talent pool out there seems very shallow when you try to replace lawyers you've lost or when you are trying to grow

- Difficult Partners drain Management's time

- Lawyers do things their way, with workarounds, so Business Support are constantly fighting fires and fighting a losing battle

- Changes outside your firm and outside your control can adversely impact part or all of your business. Your budgeting can go out the window due to no fault on your part. Due to Government tax changes, for example.

As I say, the waters are constantly choppy in a law firm. What an almighty task it is for the leadership team in a law firm to keep the ship not only right and stable through the multiple storms, but also to keep powering the ship forward. And it has to power forward. If it doesn't, the currents and headwinds drive it backwards and towards the ever-present rocks.

At least the leaders and leadership team are not alone. At least they've got the firm's Partners on their side, all doing all the right things, all the time, and all pushing things in the right direction. That's what Partners do, isn't it?

Let's see. First, we need to ask a basic question of Partners. Put simply, are they made of "The Right Stuff"?

CHAPTER 3

THE RIGHT STUFF

When beginning to explore what "The Right Stuff" is, in relation to a law firm's Partners, in my view there is a first, absolute requirement. They have to be honest.

I mean, really honest. Not just honest in that they don't steal from clients. I mean honest in terms such as:

- Refusing to certify a photocopy of their best friend's passport as being a true copy of the original, on the grounds that the original wasn't to hand

- Refusing to witness their own spouse's signature, on the grounds that the spouse had signed the document before the solicitor came into the room

- If you are in a jurisdiction that has VAT or some other sales tax, reacting properly when a client asks you to include the time spent on their *personal* legal matters in the next invoice to their *company*, so that the company can reclaim the VAT on your fees

- Reacting properly when a commercial client asks you (for tax or cashflow reasons) to invoice

Company A instead of Company B, even though the advice was given to Company B

I put this requirement so highly because of my deeply-held view of the role of law firms and lawyers in society. On one level, it is to us that clients turn for some of the biggest things in their lives. Often, these are traumatic things. If we can't help them, who can?

We are often the client's last chance to get redress, explanations, or protection from the state or from human or corporate bullies. As lawyers, if we can't stand this heat, we need to get out of this kitchen.

On another level, though, to function properly, that same society needs one guarantee of truth and honesty in the myriad transactions and relationships that make up that society.

That is where law firms come in. Someone has to always tell the truth and be honest. That's us. If Partners in a law firm aren't fastidiously honest, who can society rely on?

Interestingly, when I discussed the above examples with other people, I got two types of reaction. Law firm Partners that I spoke to looked at me completely reactionless. Of course, you have to refuse in all those cases. Non-lawyers I spoke to thought I was being ridiculously pedantic.

Moving on a step, let's examine how the Perfect Partner deals with and engages and interacts with their Partners in the firm. As you will see, the "honesty" thread is woven into this aspect, too.

In looking at what Partners and the partnership are entitled to expect from all Partners in the firm, let's look at this question by considering a very *imperfect* legal business.

I have in mind, here, a law firm where none of the pillars of the perfect legal business that I'll be bringing in later are present. Here, the Partners and their personally-owned client banks are islands and they operate in silos. Terrible, idiosyncratic behaviours abound. Business disciplines are made up as the firm goes along, where Partners can choose to charge clients or not, can set their own prices, can hold the firm back from chasing "good" clients for payment, and where there is no cross-selling or cross-caring. So, an awful (but far from rare!) position for a law firm to be in.

Even here, though, we can start building up what a Perfect Partner looks like in the eyes of the other Partners and in the eyes of the partnership as a whole. We will, in due course, layer this picture up to produce an even better version of a Partner (and address the business shortcomings just listed), but the truth is that being a Partner in a professional services firm has some immediate and universal requirements that are unrelated to the size, efficiency, success, ambitions, or trajectory of a firm.

Whilst you can argue that there are "Partners" and there are "Partners", here I am going to treat all "Partners" the same. As you will see, they all *have* to be treated the same.

Whether you are a full Equity Partner or a Fixed Share Equity Partner (and therefore an owner of part of the business), or you are an employed Salaried Partner, or you are part of the Business Support side of the business but are called or treated as a Partner, what I have to say here applies. It also applies if you happen to be called a "director" rather than "Partner" because your law firm is a limited company.

In all of these cases, you are the top tier, and you are very much *seen* as the top tier in the firm. You set the tone. You dictate the culture. You deal with the biggest things that come into the firm, crop up within the firm, or that affect the firm.

It is by others within and outside the firm looking at you – looking at you individually and collectively – that the firm will be judged as an organisation, as a law firm, and as an employer. Clients and employees and suppliers don't split hairs – if you are "a Partner", you are a Partner.

Externally, once you are a Partner in a firm, you are the firm's ambassador wherever you go, both in and out of "work". You tell the internal and external worlds everything they need to know about your partnership.

What you do and how you do it will inform the team's and the public's view of your firm. Therefore, you have a responsibility to all the other Partners and to the partnership as a whole.

Personal matters that take place "out there" (in a Partner's private life) are not taking place on a separate planet. They can have an adverse impact on the firm. Criminal convictions are one example. Holding political views and being vocal about them might be another. Being a Partner in a law firm isn't something that you walk away from each evening and return to each morning.

In bygone days, a partnership became known as a "firm" because it involved a very *firm* bond and promise between the Partners in the business. Having been a Partner in firms, I get that, and I believe I know what it means. The duty of the utmost good faith between Partners is enshrined in law.

Even though time and times have moved on, and even though we now have firms that are so large that even Equity Partners don't know each other, I believe that the need for this bond and promise between Partners is not just healthy, but is still vital.

If you were starting a law firm from scratch today (and plenty of people are), your first decision would be whether you go it alone or you set it up with someone else – with your first Partner or Partners. Above, I mentioned the exercise I do with teams of lawyers, and it is very interesting to watch as the scales fall from their eyes.

I ask them: "Would you set up a law firm with these people?" The answer is always "yes". Okay – let's look at the next stage. To get your new law firm up and running, you will either have to put a lot of your own money in, or you will have to borrow money from the bank.

If you are using the bank's money, you will either have borrowed it personally and loaned it to the business, or your business will have borrowed it, but you will have probably signed a Personal Guarantee to underwrite the loan. That Personal Guarantee might even be backed by a charge over your home. Now, ask yourself how well you *really* know the people with whom you have set up the business, any one of whom can literally do something that might mean you lose your home.

Sound ridiculous? It's not far-fetched at all.

The damage a Partner can do to a law firm goes way beyond losing fees or getting a bit of bad press for the firm after, say, a drink-driving or drunk-and-disorderly conviction.

It doesn't take many professional negligence claims caused by a careless/rogue Partner for Professional Indemnity insurers to run a mile from you come the next renewal date.

And see how you get on with an overdraft renewal or any new funding need (to cover, for example, IT upgrades, office fit-outs, tax loans, or Professional Indemnity premiums) if you need to say that you have a Partner who has been convicted of a criminal offence or a Partner who has entered into a voluntary arrangement because of the state of their personal finances.

Being a Partner, therefore, isn't a part-time job. It's not a job at all. It's a way of life. And this doesn't always sit well with some Partners, such as those who feel, "I'm a Partner – I'm not answerable to anyone".

My view is that all Partners are indeed answerable to the law firm and to the partnership on a wide range of things – including out-of-the-office things in so far as they could impact the good name and the revenues of the business. All of this means that Partners' private lives and private behaviours are affected by their being a Partner.

I also believe this requires a certain approach by Partners if and when it comes to the partnership as a whole (usually in the form of the Managing Partner) raising any enquiry of a Partner regarding any matter about which the partnership might reasonably be concerned.

On the one hand, I have myself been called to meetings about things I have done. I can say without fear of contradiction that wherever I was involved in any such discussions, I was immediately 100% cooperative and open and helpful. Perhaps because none of the issues were serious, but almost certainly because of my open and immediate response, all the issues were quickly resolved or went away.

On the other hand, there can be a different Partner response. Over the years and at multiple firms, including in my Management Consultancy life, I have seen and dealt with an incredibly wide array of issues where engagement with an individual Partner was necessary. Partner responses fell into two camps – those who were immediately open and fully cooperative, and those who were closed and evasive and unhelpful.

Doing something wrong is not the end of the world – we've all done it. Making Management's job harder by being unhelpful, or by being resentful at the intrusion, or worse – by lying – is not going to help the firm to protect its name and business. I do not believe any Partner who adopts this response is deserving of the partnership's support.

It is often the unhelpful response, rather than the behaviour or incident in question, that really represents the breach of the deep-seated trust that needs to exist between all Partners.

In the new law firm we have been referring to, what a Partner of yours does (or fails to do) might not mean you lose your home. But, each and every Partner in a firm is capable of undermining the firm's good name, the hard work of its people, and its income levels.

This can all happen with the best will in the world and absent any deliberate act on the part of a Partner. Where that changes for the worse is where there is a deliberate act not to engage with or cooperate with the partnership and its Management to help reduce the impact of the events in question.

As does every leader of a law firm, or of a team within a law firm, I had Partners bring sometimes difficult personal or professional issues to me, where we and others in the partnership worked together and were able to steer the situation to the best possible outcome.

We stood by the Partner.

Yes, they might have made a mistake or an error of judgement of some sort, but – as I say – haven't we all? What they had then done, though, was to respect and indeed reinforce the trust and the bond between Partners in a partnership. Compare that to a Partner who is evasive or who tries to lie their way out of a situation. To my mind, a Partner has to be trustworthy *all the time*, or they are not trustworthy any of the time.

Above, I used the words: "I'm a Partner – I'm not answerable to anyone". You cannot think of yourself being a Partner, but at the same time being an island. If you want that, be a barrister or a sole practitioner.

Being a Partner means being a team member, where the team is the partnership. It is bigger than you. It governs you, you don't govern it, even if you are one of its owners. It is entitled to lay down requirements of you and, of course, you will hopefully do well out of it.

Some partnerships have no rules. I'm not referring to a written legal document like a partnership agreement or a shareholders' agreement. I mean rules that relate to how the place operates as an organisation, law firm, employer, and business.

Here, there is no recognised and embraced "way" that the firm does things. They can literally be a group of self-governing individuals where everyone can do what they want, their way. That can bring a wide range of issues and business challenges. It is also a wasted opportunity. If only it had its way of operating, a set of rules and rails that governed everyone and everything (though in an adult way rather than in a "micro-management" kind of way). The result would be short- and medium- and long-term business success, a long-term future for its people, and an admirable legacy for the Partners.

As you will see from this book, and the others in this trilogy, I am strongly in favour of there being such a "way" – a handful of *rules and rails that apply to everyone in the firm*, including Partners.

That would, of course, require the Partners to come together and agree on what the rules were going to be. From time to time within a partnership – be it weekly, monthly, quarterly, or annually – the Partners in a firm do (or should!) come together. But let's be honest, are such coming-togethers really going to secure what the firm needs?

CHAPTER 4
PARTNERS MEETINGS

Partners coming together to discuss matters affecting the firm is not widely celebrated as a mechanism that brings agility and action. Businesses "out there" don't point to law firm partnerships and say, "We need to be more like them".

Whilst we can build a clear picture of what is needed for a law firm to thrive sustainably, and whilst we can see – in particular – what is needed from a law firm's Partners to keep it thriving, converting that clarity into action on the ground is easier said than done.

I'm often told, "Simon, these things that you talk about – we get it and we love it. But the minute you walk out of here, the wheels will come off. We know what to do – we just can't implement it, and we definitely can't stick at things". The reason for this (in a nutshell) is the nature of Partner meetings – the formal and informal interactions between Partners in a firm where decisions can be made and need to be made. Decisions, the ability to make them, and the ability to be agile are all vital business tools.

As a junior lawyer, I'd long wondered what Partners meetings were like. They seemed to be of vital importance, and being entitled to go to them appeared to be the ultimate badge of importance.

What they are actually like depends on a range of things. Let me look at a few types, as this in itself will tell us something about what the business needs from its Partners to change even an already-successful firm's trajectory for the better.

In a big firm that is run by a CEO or Managing Partner, Partners meetings are a useful way of communicating and taking soundings. They can be something of a formality. By definition, in such firms, there will almost certainly be a Strategy and a Business Plan in place that Management is pushing, and the expectation is that all the Partners will do their bit to do the same. Some Partners might not even go to these meetings, and many who do go will sit there and say nothing. Such meetings are not theatres where collaboration or innovation shine.

Perfect Partners here, in the eyes of Management, are those who are rowing hard in the direction that the Strategy document requires them to (which usually means "doing lots of billing"), and those who are not rocking the boat.

These meetings follow a path, and they rarely explode into conflict. A lot of Partners in such meetings just keep their heads down. Many Partners do not find these meetings uplifting. Managing Partners complain that they get nothing back from their Partners in such meetings.

Smaller Partners meetings are different. These could be small because the firm is smaller, or because they are meetings of, for example, just the Equity Partners in a firm, or they are meetings of the Partners in a particular office, or of the Partners for a specific team within a large firm.

Partner behaviours at these smaller meetings can be very different. Partners can now do what they do best and what they are paid to do – that is to talk and argue. Listen? All too often, no. Partners can be sat simply waiting for their turn to speak, not listening to what anyone else is saying.

In literally hundreds of Partner meetings that I have watched and been part of (at dozens of firms), I have seen the issue to be dealt with quickly lost.

Instead, there are multi-level discussions where Partners craft clever, point-scoring arguments, often transparently based around their own self-interests or penchants or people. I constantly have to bring such meetings back to the key issues that the meeting started off discussing.

Partners don't seem to realise that it is in these meetings that things can happen and that real progress can be made, or that things cannot happen and progress is not made. The Partners are directly the cause of the former or the latter. What they should see is that decision-making is a key competitive advantage, and that all their competitors are similarly getting bogged down in unproductive meetings. A law firm's real opportunity is borne of the fact that all its competitors are law firms!

Compare a law firm Partners meeting with a meeting being held by, say, the directors of an IT company or an engineering business. Paralysis on the one hand, and agility and fleetness of foot on the other.

And not only do decisions not get made enough in law firm meetings, but such meetings actually sap the will to live in their attendees. The meetings themselves become feared. They are not the place to inject energy and impetus to a legal business (which they could easily be), but rather are something to be dreaded and (if possible) avoided. The interviews I carried out in the course of writing this book (see later on) give an idea of what law firm Partner meetings feel like to the people running law firms.

There seems to be a desire on the part of Partners to get involved in minutiae, and an unwillingness to say, "This isn't that important to me – you decide. If it doesn't work, we can try something else". Items that are important, but not addressed, are left to be carried over to the next meeting.

I am often flabbergasted at what Partner meetings will focus on. It's often trivia at a time when, for example, a firm or team might have £1m in unpaid bills on which they've paid VAT of £200,000, or staff might be leaving because one of the Partners is horrible. It's insanity. But point scoring and "having your say" are put above such life and death issues.

These behaviours are in lawyers' DNA. We "do" detail, but that can mean that we don't see bigger pictures. It's just the way we think and, as a consequence, we get bogged down in minutiae. Let it go! We need some self-awareness and – frankly – an ability to laugh at ourselves. The outside business world would certainly laugh at us as they make entrepreneurial decisions by the bucket-load.

In my second book – "The Perfect Lawyer" – I discuss how such meetings can hold law firms back, and the root cause is that Partners feel entitled to have their say on *everything*. All it takes is one Partner to adopt a contrary position. Leadership of the meeting is not usually robust or powerful enough to say, "Thank you, we've listened to your views, but we need to make a decision, so we'll go with X. If it doesn't work, we'll bring it back to the meeting, but well done us for showing decision-making agility."

Usually, the non-Partners in, for example, a team or department meeting are sat there thinking, "I'm a lawyer, get me out of here". Does anyone ever look around the room and add up the cost of the meeting?

I think an inability to make decisions, when a group of Partners argue over everything or talk things to death, is something to be ashamed of. Yes, ashamed. Why do I say that? I say it because a firm is the source of financial well-being for many more people than the highly-paid Partners at the meeting.

Many, or dozens, or even hundreds of mortgages and household incomes depend on that business ploughing through the waves that are being caused by what I genuinely believe to be a worsening storm for law firms.

Partners should bury any views they harbour on matters that are materially less important than keeping the law firm – in reputation, profit, employer, and cash terms – on the straight and narrow and powering forward. Just let stuff go; it's not that important.

There are times when I see a Partner in a firm being negative or difficult, only for it to turn out that whilst they are throwing a spanner in the works, the data shows that their own performance and contribution to the business are both highly questionable. As a profession, we seem to have a blind spot when it comes to elephants.

Instead of dwelling on minutiae, Partners should look at the key issues instead, the elephants in the room, often starting in their own backyards:

- How much of my day am I giving to clients for free because I only record about 3 or 4 hours a day?

- What hourly rate am I actually recovering, when you divide my annual billings by the number of hours I have recorded, let alone done? (The figure is often shockingly low.)

- What is the *cash* impact of myself and the team I'm in? (If you look under the "billings" bonnet, the cash impact of a "successful" team can be truly awful. Did you see in my first book the Team Cash Impact Statements I used? Horrifying!)

- Are there files in our team that we are just not getting around to working on?

- If there are such files, why are we having meetings about marketing?

- How many lawyers have left our team in the last two years, and why?

- And why are we struggling to replace them?

- How many of our other teams are doing work for the clients that we act for?

- Why aren't we getting exposure to the clients of those other teams?

These questions are what Partners meetings should be about. Partners may feel that Partners are top of the pile, but they still need to look up. And I don't mean look up to the CEO or the Managing Partner. The thing is that, in a law firm, everyone has a boss. Even the Managing Partner or the CEO, or the Board – everyone has a boss that they are to serve by using their best endeavours to give it what it needs. Who is this boss? The *business* is the boss. That boss will be around a long time after all the Partners have come and gone.

What that boss needs is in the name – *business*. It needs profit, and more importantly, it needs cash. And it needs more of both every year. An obsession with just those things, though, could lead to an organisation being brutal and greedy and "short-termist". History is littered with the carcasses of such firms.

So what is needed from all the Partners is an obsession with *profit and cash in a sustainable and growing fashion.*

"Sustainable" is the element that requires a wider range of priorities than just a Partner's obsession with hitting this year's personal billing target.

In my experience, the vast majority of resources in law firms, partnerships, and Partner meetings do not focus on the "sustainable, etc" obsession that we need to focus on. Partners, who are the key to generating and growing the requisite profit and cash growth in the medium and long terms, are typically involved in so many other short-term, time-consuming, energy-consuming, often expensive exercises, obsessions, and projects that steer a firm's resources away from these key pillars of a legal business. Generating profit and cash in a sustainable and growing way is the rubber on the tyres, or the needle on the record, and yet this need is all too often skated over.

Supremely, Partners are people who are in business together. They are not in a talking shop together. They are in a boat together – along with a lot of other people who are equally important. And it's not a boat that will automatically stay afloat forever.

I have seen Partners stop rowing and turn around in the boat to argue with other crew, and even start drilling holes in the boat, when all the time they should be rowing hard and in the same direction.

The boat just staying afloat is not an option – it needs to be moving forward, and fast. Moving forward slowly is no longer good enough, as the water itself is moving backwards and the problems are being made worse by headwinds. The walls are closing in on the sector. How? Client needs are changing, prices are being challenged, Direct and Indirect Costs are going through the roof, Artificial Intelligence is knocking on our doors (and will soon be kicking the doors in), and the mobility of lawyers and Business Support staff has reached levels that make it very, very hard to actually run – let alone grow – a law firm.

It beggars belief what law firms (that is, Partners) think are important issues, when under their noses there are these existential threats.

"Let's carry on spending hours discussing whether we sponsor the local food or jazz festival again", when, in effect, a firm's lawyers might literally be giving away half of all the work they do for clients.

To be Perfect Partners in all they do, Partners need to put all the factors that bring "profit and cash in a sustainable and growing fashion" first. As the GB Rowing Team asked at the Olympics, when they felt there was too much non-core activity going on around them, "Does it make the boat go faster?" Partners should be asking the same question. If it doesn't make the boat go faster, ditch it and don't waste time and energy discussing it. Instead, identify and focus on the things that will make the boat go faster in terms of sustainably growing profit and cash.

Perhaps a useful step forward here is for Partners to realise that a positive change in a law firm's trajectory is entirely possible, and the keys to that change are in their hands. All that is needed is for the Partners – individually and collectively – to listen, focus, and to then stay on the right rails.

Pausing there – in looking at what makes a Perfect Partner – we can summarise three things on the list so far:

1. They have to be made of The Right Stuff, particularly in terms of honesty and trustworthiness, and in terms of openness with their Partners

2. They have to aid and lubricate the decision-making process in a firm, not throw sand in the engine. They need to add to, not detract from, a firm's agility

3. They have to be focused on the right priorities

Let's drill a bit deeper into the last of these points to examine what the boss (i.e., the business) actually needs from a Partner in terms of their direct and hard contribution to the ongoing success of the firm.

It needs much more than this direct, hard contribution – as we will see – but when all is said and done, each Partner does have to bring value to the table.

CHAPTER 5

A PARTNER'S DIRECT CONTRIBUTION TO THE BUSINESS

Over the decades of being in private practise, and later being a legal sector Management Consultant, I have seen under the bonnet of many different law firms around the world. I have seen the range of things that law firms and partnerships require and expect from their Partners in terms of their explicit contribution to the business. Their performance against these requirements is usually directly linked to their reward and their share of the profits.

Across a wide range of firms, I have never seen a profit-share and partner-assessment structure that works to *all* of the Partners' satisfaction, particularly as a firm changes and grows.

The ideal would be a system where all Partners contributed to the business equally and shared profits equally. That would rid a firm of the difficult discussions that are had each year, and the many hours of Partner time spent behind closed doors, discussing why Partner X got more points and, therefore, more money, than Partner Y. However, being lawyers and high-achievers, it's hard getting lawyers to accept – over the long term – that all Partners' contributions can be equal or that they are in fact equal (particularly as a firm grows and evolves and new Partners join the partnership from both inside and outside the firm).

Some firms have a very narrow requirement, where a Partner's personal billing simply needs to be at a certain level. Often, the Partner's reward (in terms of what share of the firm's profits they get at year-end) will hinge on whether they have hit the required personal fee levels.

So, of course, where your reward depends on your personal fees, that is exactly what you'll focus on, isn't it? Do other stuff to help the firm? You're joking!

A slightly broader version of this is where a Partner's reward depends on not only their own fees but also the level of fees *across the firm* that is directly attributable to them. Here, it can be of value to a Partner if they are responsible for client relationships where the clients instruct (and pay) a range of lawyers in the firm, possibly across a range of teams.

The devil is in the detail, of course, and putting to one side the fact that arguments can easily develop over precisely how a client came to be a client of the firm (and who, therefore, gets the credit for that client's billings) I think that this is a better way to go in business and business growth terms than the direct-personal-billings model. It, at least, rewards Partners for acquiring brand new clients for other teams, and for developing existing small clients into big clients for the whole firm. It encourages Partners to ensure that clients are looked after so that they stay with the firm, and it encourages Partners to introduce clients to more and more teams across the firm. It reduces what I call 'silo-think'.

Even this, though, is not without its challenges. The introducing Partner needs to be able to trust lawyers across the firm – not just in terms of delivering a great service to clients that are introduced to them, but also in terms of not trying to take the client's billings when it comes to year-end profit-share discussions. And what if Partner A raises lots of bills to Partner B's clients? Does Partner B get all the credit? If so, if I was Partner A, I'd focus on my own clients instead of those introduced to me by other Partners in the firm.

So far, in this chapter, all we've talked about is billing. I do think, however, that in terms of a hard, direct contribution to the business, there are other inputs that can be made (and that need to be made) by Partners.

Let me give you an example. Me.

As a fee-earning junior lawyer, my billing in the early 1990s approached £100,000 per year. It wasn't a stellar performance, and in many firms I simply would not have secured promotion to partnership based on my billing levels. I had left firms that insisted on a contribution that was limited to my personal billings. In light of what was to come, that was a huge loss to those firms.

I had other skills and other interests, namely the business of law and the marketing of legal services. None of this would have got me anywhere at most firms. Thankfully, the firm I was in (Pannone) had an amazing Managing Partner, who saw something that could be of much greater value to the business. Joy Kingsley engaged with me and asked whether I'd be interested in focusing on "marketing" instead of fees, as she could see I had both the skills and a keen interest in that area.

She told me it would enhance my career progression, not hold it back. I trusted her and leapt at the chance.

I delivered, and Joy and the Partners delivered. Based on my Business Development results, rather than my billing figures (as I was now billing precisely zero), I was promoted to Salaried Partner a short while later. My billing performance would never have got me there. A while later, to the enormous credit again of Joy and of the entire Equity Partnership in the firm, I joined the ownership group as a non-fee-earning Equity Partner – an extremely rare thing in the 90s (and perhaps a rare thing even now).

They didn't all vote me in because I'm a nice guy, although I really am. They did it because there was hard business success in there. They trusted me to do my bit for the business, in my way. Many of my results were measurable in monetary terms. I can honestly say that I brought many, many £millions of fees into the firm. That eclipsed any billing I could have done in even a lifetime of lawyering. Some of my results were not so easily measurable – raising our profile and making sure we were visible "out there", helping other teams and lawyers with their Business Development activity, and so on.

In its simplest form, I can look back to a long string of very lucrative Business Development successes that I had in attracting brand new clients which were of the "networking" and "relationship-building" variety. I simply would not have been able to do that if I had been carrying the weight of chargeable hours or a billing target around my neck. I'd have done the minimum, turning up at events and showing my face before rushing back to the office to record more time on files. The same goes for taking time to visit large companies that were then small clients of the firm. I have so many stories of companies that had used us in the past for the smallest thing, but who – with the investment of time by me – were nurtured and developed into big users of our lawyers across the firm. Later in this book, I look at Partner-level Business Development in more detail.

My contribution was not billing, therefore, but other people's billing. I learned from this, and both in that firm and when I became Managing Partner at another firm, I similarly elevated and encouraged lawyers to do the same, to good effect.

So, it's not all about billing. And nor is it all about lawyers delivering law to clients. What about the Partner who is responsible for overseeing and managing risk and compliance in a firm? Without them, the lights could go out.

And what about the Marketing and HR and Training and IT Partners? Having a flow of new clients, great people who are getting greater, all with great systems to work on, are all truly priceless dimensions to a law firm. A Partner's *billing* can pale next to these contributions.

And the Managing Partner or CEO or Managing Director? I still have Partners telling me that they think their firm's Managing Partner should have a personal billing target. The Partners saying that have obviously never been at the helm of a law firm, let alone a large one. Not only is it a monumentally time-consuming role (particularly if you do all the "people" and all the "leadership" things right), but also doing those things right can transform the performance and outlook of a firm more than any individual fee-earning Partner ever could. Should they really have a workload and a billing target? Absolutely not!

And what of middle management – the Team Leaders and Heads of Department? Do we need big fees from them personally? Again, I say "No!", as by properly leading and growing a team and getting the team's performance up (and we come to all of these things later in this book) they can make a difference that again leaves in the shade anything that their personal billing might ever be able to achieve.

So when we look at what hard and direct contribution we need a Partner to make to the law firm, the fact is that (as we will see) there are four legs to the law firm stool. Billing and "money" is just one of them. The law firm graveyard is full of firms that focused on that one leg of the stool alone in order to make maximum money as quickly as possible. Partner contributions are needed to strengthen each of the four legs of the stool. These contributions can be from lawyer Partners who assume varied roles, or they can be Business Support colleagues who attain the status of Partners in the firm.

It's not my saying, but it is very graphic and clear: "If Senior Management only reward fish for climbing trees, that's what the fish will focus on".

If a law firm only rewards personal billing, it might miss out on the benefits that could come from getting Partners to do something they might be much better at.

And of course, it's a spiral upwards. Get people doing what they're best at, reward them, get all the great people in different roles and making different contributions working as a team, and watch them attain even higher heights together.

And by "heights", I really am thinking high…

CHAPTER 6

MOONSHOT

I can't exaggerate the heights that are attainable, or the extent of the possible change in law firms if the Partners all adopt and adapt to – individually and collectively – a number of priorities and disciplines. We are talking "destiny" here, not just "making more money".

Year in and year out, many law firms set budgets for the year ahead, hoping to move forward a bit and maybe secure an increase in turnover of 5-10%. That then gets broken down into team and personal billing targets. Law firm leaders and their Finance Directors have their annual, fractious discussions with Team Leaders about what the teams could and should produce in terms of billing, and individual lawyers revolt when their billing target is more than three times their salary.

That is a typical scenario. It means hundreds – thousands – of law firms are in a steady orbit around Planet Norm, where nothing really exciting can happen. Fuel (money, time, energy) is being consumed at a heck of a rate to keep the firm circling. Have you ever seen a picture of all the satellites and spaceships that are circling Earth right now? That's exactly what the legal sector looks like.

And everyone will be doing the same thing next year, and the year after (providing, of course, the orbiting firm doesn't succumb to the pull of gravity that is the ever-increasing rise of costs and the ever-increasing monthly and annual cash needs of law firms).

There is a way to break out of this orbit. Until the Apollo 8 space mission in the 1960s, all that "spacecraft" had ever done was go up a bit, turn left, and start going round and round Earth.

They never actually went into space. They stayed in Earth's orbit. Apollo 8, though, did something very different. It was the first rocket to apply full power so that instead of continually orbiting our planet, held there by Earth's gravity, at a certain point it powered up and it went straight on, escaping the pull of Earth's gravity. It went out into space and towards the Moon. "TLI" they called it – Trans Lunar Injection.

Law firms could do with a bit of TLI – the application of full organisational power so that the old gravitational bonds of tradition and inertia and custom and habit are broken and a new destiny is set. A law firm can indeed free itself of the pull of Planet Norm's gravity, and head off in a new direction. It's not actually the Moon we want to get to. There is no destination on this journey. It's more about a fantastic journey amongst the stars.

And how do you start that amazing journey to the stars? You need rails! Yes, rails. That is, a firm needs to:

- Choose the right rails to get on
- Have the whole firm stay on those rails

- Ensure the Partners (individually and collectively) drive the firm along those rails

- Maximise the presence and impact of what I call the "magic ingredient" that will help a firm to get its hands on the real glittering prize that is available here

One size does not fit all. Nor does Management just throwing a set of rails at people get the firm anywhere. The firm, and the teams in it, need to design their own rails. The chosen rails will depend on things like the work of a team, or its marketplace, or its clients. There are some rails that are of fundamental importance to any successful, sustainably-growing legal business, and I set those out in this book.

Any right-thinking team or firm ought to adopt (and if need be, adapt) them, and also to add their own rails to the mix.

It is the Partners, though, that the spotlight remains on. They need to embrace the project and then push and guide the firm along the rails, all the time. It is also the Partners who add – or remove – the "magic ingredient" that will change the game.

Let's now start bringing the rails out into the sunlight.

CHAPTER 7

THE FOUR-LEGGED STOOL

Even if a Partner embraces all that I have looked at so far, it's not enough. Partners can be as honest as the day is long, and 100% trustworthy, but if Partners don't do what is needed to get the business onto the right rails, and then keep the business moving along those rails, no one else can fill that gap. It just won't happen.

No highly-driven Managing Partner, and no dedicated and growing Business Support team can, in place of the Partners, do what is needed. The former is all too often a "Manager of Partners" rather than a visionary, thrusting agent of change. The dreams and plans they harboured when they started out in the hot seat can disappear as the daily grind of herding strong-willed and highly opinionated Partners takes over. The latter universally complain of having to spend their lives tidying up after those Partners who seem to think the rules don't apply to them.

Partners need to come together to overcome the challenges that can get in the way of progress, and they need to agree on a set of overarching rails that they all embrace and that can then be taken out to the teams in the firm for their input and polishing.

The rails must strengthen each leg of the four-legged stool that is a law firm. With all four legs strong, the firm will itself remain strong in even a howling gale. Weaken one leg, and the end is nigh.

The four legs that need to be strong to bring sustainable growth of the right type to a law firm are the four C's:

- Colleagues – we need great people, who are made greater, who stay because they love the culture of the firm, who perform highly, and who deliver exactly what the business needs

- Clients – we need good clients to whom we deliver outstanding care, who want to use us for everything that we offer, who are happy to agree a good price for doing so, and who actually pay their bills

- Compliance – you can literally have your firm shut down now, and you can go to prison or – at the very least – face hefty fines and damaging publicity. Risk is everywhere. It needs to be actively managed, not ranked in importance behind a day at the races.

- Cash – we need literally tons of the stuff. All the time. And more next year than we needed this year.

Looking back at the earlier chapter where we discussed direct Partner contributions to the business, you can now see the range of Partner contributions to a law firm that are of real value. It cannot be all about the Partners' billing. The Partners can and must help to strengthen all four legs of the stool. A weak leg anywhere can be fatal.

These are the four facets of a law firm that need protecting and promoting, and out of which our rails will be borne. Partners in a law firm, of course, have a vested interest in doing this protecting and promoting – whether you're already an Equity Partner or you're a Salaried Partner who needs the cake to grow so that there's room at the Equity table for you in due course.

Partners in a law firm have a direct, exacting, and constant responsibility to discharge in ensuring each of these legs of the stool is strong and that the rails that are borne out of them remain central to all that a firm and its people do. And it is the people that we will look at first – the "Colleagues" leg of the stool.

CHAPTER 8

COLLEAGUES

Let's look at the first "Colleagues" leg of the stool. Junior lawyers are a key constituency of a firm, and they have needs of the Partners in a firm. Indeed, the satisfaction of those needs is vital. If you can't retain junior lawyers, your business will be in constant turmoil, and the brand and profitability will erode. Any particular team that cannot keep its junior lawyers will shrink, and the firm as a whole will be challenged.

Why would junior lawyers stay at a firm? The answer is a mix of reward, progression, opportunities, quality of work, pride in the team's and the firm's purpose, and – critically – the judgement that they make around the firm's culture. Culture here means "What is the experience of working here really like?" Literally – "How does it make me feel?"

In reality, because Partners hold the power in a firm, this means "How do the Partners make me feel?" Going even further, it means "How do the Partners I actually work with make me feel?"

There are some soft aspects to a firm delivering 'the necessary' here, and some hard aspects. The hard aspects are money, career path, effective and authentic appraisals, and an active plan to develop and progress every person in the firm. The softer aspects are more human and they boil down, I believe, to these two questions:

1. What are the Partners that I work with like? How do they make me feel?

2. Are all Partners in the firm the same?

    a. Is there a behavioural floor below which no Partner is allowed to go, or are some questionable (or worse) behaviours tolerated?

    b. Is there a clear (and good) "way" that the Partners in my firm behave and operate?

    c. Does a lawyer's experience at the firm depend on which team or office you are in? If yes, then clearly there is no firm-wide culture – there are, instead, local cultures that evade any policing where Partners can behave how they want.

From a junior lawyer's perspective, we saw what "bad" can look like in Chapter 1. The notes later in this book of the conversations I have had with people around this question are, frankly, horrifying.

Let's have a look at what "good" looks like.

The work that lawyers at every level routinely carry out is usually one of the most important things in a client's life at that time. Clients are inevitably anxious and often fired up, and thus, they are capable of responding out of character. We usually talk about things that might have immense financial and possibly emotional value.

Clients' guards will be up. Sensitivities are high. Dealing with these things as a lawyer is not an easy job.

And it can get worse for a junior lawyer. There is a robust and demanding regulatory framework in law firms that kicks in at the first whiff of a complaint from a client. There are plenty of lawyers out there who will take over cases and (with or without good grounds) put the boot into the former lawyer. That could be to pull the client out from under an unpaid bill or as part of a claim the client wants to now bring for professional negligence.

All of this can land in the lap of junior lawyers who are doing their best at a time when they usually have a large caseload made up of many such demanding, anxious clients. Expecting junior lawyers to take these things in their stride is unreasonable.

When mud is thrown at a junior lawyer, it is a significant moment for that lawyer. At the very least, it will bring worry and stress. It might bring fear that the lawyer's otherwise good work and progress in the firm might be undermined. It could be a career setback.

It could be what we can call a "vague" complaint, borne out of unhappiness on the part of a client with something on the case where no real harm was done.

Or it could be what we can call a "concrete" complaint, where the client (or their new lawyer) can point to material loss or damage caused by a certain action or inaction by the junior lawyer.

In my career as a fee-earner, I was guilty of both vague and concrete "offences".

Whichever it is, at that moment, the junior lawyer needs support. And they need to feel supported. That is – they need support from, and to be supported by, the Partners around them.

As a recently qualified solicitor, this very thing happened to me. It wouldn't happen now, but back then I was a Commercial Litigator and I also did any Corporate Defence work (such as defending clients who faced Trading Standards prosecutions, etc.) and any Criminal Defence work where the directors of our corporate clients were charged with criminal offences in their personal or business lives.

We had one such director client who was charged with a dishonesty offence, and the case was passed to me. It didn't go well, to put it mildly.

When the director was convicted after a Not Guilty plea in a Crown Court jury trial, he sacked me and went to an absolute Rottweiler of a lawyer (a Partner) at another firm, whom he instructed to go after me. The new lawyer didn't need much encouragement.

The first I heard of it was a visit from the Head of Litigation, the Partner who was – at that time – my Team Leader. My jaw hit the desk. My heart sank.

The complaint from the new lawyer was that I had badly advised a gentleman of impeccable character, that this was a minor offence that should never have got anywhere near a Crown Court, and that if it had been kept down in the Magistrates Court, it would all have blown away.

As it was, it was now being said that the client – because of me – had a Crown Court conviction against his name and was facing (much greater) Crown Court sentencing powers. The new lawyer demanded a meeting with me and the Partner who was in charge of me.

Ahead of the meeting, the Partner went through the file with me in detail. He invested real time with me in getting things ready for the meeting. Then we went to the meeting in a conference room downstairs. I will never forget the violent outpouring of poison and vitriol from the new lawyer. It was absolutely vicious. It took my breath away. I felt physically sick.

The Partner in charge of me, who had up to this point sat in silence, let him finish and then spoke briefly to the new lawyer: "I'm going to hand you two things, and then you are going to leave our offices. First, here's a copy of your client's criminal record, in which you will see numerous dishonesty and other convictions.

"Second, here's a note of the hearing in the Magistrates Court in this case when the Magistrates accepted the Prosecution's invitation to them that they decline jurisdiction on the matter because they believed your client was the centre of a major crime ring. This meeting is over, so please leave our offices now."

Yes! That's what Partners do to stand behind their junior lawyers! Compare that to the awful Partner behaviour set out in Chapter 1.

I learned from this and I "paid it on", as they say, when I was a Partner. I recall when I saw one of our junior lawyers literally run out of her office looking ashen-faced and then turn and run back into her office. I knew something was wrong. I went in and asked.

The young lawyer had missed a hearing or a time limit –
I forget which – but it was something pretty black and
white. We got some of the Partners in the team
together, worked with the young lawyer to come clean
with the client and with the other side, agreed to pay
some costs, got everything back on track within the
hour, made a friend for life of the young lawyer, and
protected the firm from a negligence claim. Who do
you think learned the most there? The junior lawyer,
obviously… about coming clean, about teamwork,
about underlining key dates, and about the great culture
of the firm she was part of.

Great Partners put these things ahead of cash. Cash is
short-term value. Honour, decency, respect, humanity –
not only are these things downright good, they also
bring a long-term return and are much more valuable in
a law firm than some transitory fees.

When I was Managing Partner, I recall we had a Partner
who was head of a team in one of our offices. They had
a large client, and his team were focused on that client.
The early fees were very good, but relations with the
client quickly deteriorated. Morale in the team sank.
The lights went out in their eyes.

The Partner did the right thing and approached me
with a view to protecting his team's well-being. I had a
decision to make. Having taken a large gulp, I sacked
the client, in the full knowledge that the new team
would have no work.

Management's stock went through the roof. Stories of
such support get around a firm quickly. The team came
out fighting on the marketing and Business
Development fronts.

But it's about more than being there for junior lawyers when there is a crisis. Some Partners who will indeed be there in a crisis might, in their normal working life, be missing opportunities to spread the gold dust that Partners' pockets are full of, in other ways. Being an island shut away in an actual or imaginary office, or at home nowadays, where there is little or no engagement with junior lawyers, is a wasted opportunity to make other lawyers great. They are the future of the firm. Let's make them great!

Junior lawyers will forever remember how Partners made them feel. I can cast my mind back and still remember, literally decades later, moments where Partners made me feel big, or made me feel small. One example? As a junior lawyer, I remember fondly working with a mighty Litigation Partner on a number of huge cases. This included numerous instances of us working all night. Throughout those times, the Partner would educate and challenge me and immerse me in the cases, giving me direct client contact on what were usually highly sensitive disputes.

If that wasn't enough, after one such case, where we had both worked around the clock repeatedly, he came to me and explained that he had spoken with the Head of HR, and that he had arranged for me to get an extra £50 in my pay packet that month. That £50 felt like a £million – his gratitude and his going out of his way for me had an amazingly uplifting effect.

At another firm, literally quite by chance, we'd landed a great new client, and I became the main lawyer on their cases even though I was only two or three years qualified. One Partner from another team who I took to a meeting with that client made a point of telling me that he was there to support me (amazing!), so I should feel free to be myself and to run the meeting as I wanted. Truly uplifting.

Compare that to another Partner who invited my main contact at a client (for whom I did most, if not all, of the work) to hospitality at a football match, without involving me. The client rang me and asked if I would be there too. I said that was the first I'd heard of it. The client was appalled and refused to go. The former Partners lifted me, the latter Partner deflated me.

Being praised by a Partner for something is a big deal. Being praised by a Partner who is praising you for something another Partner has told them about is off the scale.

And it's not just *praise* that works. Good, honest, constructive feedback from a Partner is amazing when you are on the receiving end, even if it makes for uncomfortable listening.

Being told by the Partner who was in charge of the firm's Trainee Solicitors that I couldn't have the next seat that I wanted during my articles (now called the Training Contract) because the Team Leader in question thought I was – to use his precise words – "a clown" was amazingly valuable for me. It was a turning point in my professional development.

At last, I got a much-needed grip on things. That Partner could have said nothing, let time run on, and on qualification, there would have obviously been no job for me. Instead, he turned me around, and I eventually became an Equity Partner at that firm – with him!

I feel sure that, in due course, I added significantly to the firm's business over the years. What a great and constructive job he did, both for the business and for me.

You can see that what's different here is how the junior lawyer feels. It's as soft and as nebulous as that. But it's vital.

A positive, uplifting environment can be undermined by a Partner having strong relationships with some junior lawyers in a team but not with others. A Partner having "favourites" is not a great look. As you'll see later in this book, it blows away the magic ingredient that can get everything working so well. A regime where your progression depends on which team or office you are in, or which Partner you work with, is awful.

Partners having favourites and being seen to have favourites is a long way from a fair and transparent merit-based system of progression. That kind of regime does not make you feel great as a junior lawyer.

We all want to feel great and fairly-treated, so if you can't get that feeling at your current firm, you will inevitably look elsewhere for it.

Partners maybe forget what things were like before they were a Partner. Junior lawyers talk incessantly amongst themselves about the Partners around them – that's just how it is. A Partner should never think that their good or bad behaviours stay secret – everyone knows. That can be really good for a Partner or really bad. What do you think is being said about you?

One thing that is avidly mocked, of course, is "Partner-itis" – the deterioration in behaviours that afflicts many "normal" lawyers as soon as they become Partners. Attitudes worsen, entitlement can creep in, aloofness arises, and self-importance can rocket. And all these things can be fed by a lack of self-awareness.

As we'll move onto, later in this book, I have done these "people" things a disservice by referring to them in this chapter as soft and nebulous. They actually all come together with other elements in a furnace where a white-hot heat can forge an incredibly valuable business tool that brings hard business results.

That's for later, though. For now, as we carry on our journey, let's turn to the next leg of the stool, which will shine a light on the other rails that we need to have in place.

CHAPTER 9
CLIENTS

For sustainable success, we need good clients who want to use us for everything that we offer, who are willing to pay a good price for doing so, and who actually pay their bills. There is usually a mismatch, though, between what a client wants and what we want. Here's a typical client's wish list:

- I want a great lawyer…

- Preferably a heavyweight partner…

- Who knows the law superbly…

- Who fights tooth and nail for me…

- Who does what I tell them to do…

- Who communicates with me all the time…

- Who does all of that for a very low fee…

- Who won't bill me for ages…

- And who doesn't mind if I then take ages to pay that bill

This doesn't work for us. We need to have our own list of requirements. It's a two-way street. And we need to be slow to let anyone become a client of ours at all.

I still remember a friend of mine in the early 90s, when I was an Articled Clerk, saying he had a friend who was a businessman who needed a lawyer to help him with business issues. Keen as mustard, I spoke with the Partner I worked with. He listened, but then he wanted to know more. Then more. Then more. I was getting very wound up with this. So many questions! For Heaven's sake – why don't we just get the guy in and get going on his case?

The difference, of course, between the Partner and me at that time was that they had judgement, balance, and wisdom. They had radar. Over-the-horizon radar, as it turned out. This was not a client we wanted to touch. The Partner posed this question to me as a first reason to pause, "Why, if he is a successful businessman, does he not already have lawyers?"

This "radar" is a key function of Partners. Not to perennially grow client numbers at any cost and have constant "new business" wins, but to guard the gates and be very fussy about who gets in. Law firms can have their brand and good name tainted by whom they agree to act for.

With no apologies for being blunt, it helps in various areas of my work to divide whatever we happen to be looking at simply into A, B, or C.

- A is great

- B is okay

- C is unacceptable

You need to do this with clients. From tomorrow. In fact, from today. Don't let any more C clients in.

How do you know if they're a C? Well, rest assured, the following are good indicators:

- They are secretive or evasive

- Unclear in their instructions

- Unreasonably complaining

- Rude

- Blaming

- Won't agree to your high fees

- Won't part with cash

New clients can be treated with some scepticism. Why are they looking for new lawyers? What happened with the last ones they used?

For all new clients, and indeed on all new matters for existing clients, we need to have an increasingly exacting relationship with the client. That applies to reputational questions as well as compliance issues, such as anti-money laundering, etc. There are multiple "risk" issues that the firm needs its Partners to police. A firm can be laid low by a Partner taking on a case that is outside their area of expertise, because it interests them or because it offers a big fee. Believe me, I know.

This filtering should apply to reputational and risk factors, but also to *commercial* dimensions. The usual but inadequate tests that might be applied are:

- Is it an interesting case?

- Are they a big-name client?

- Will there be a big bill on the case?

- Is it an area of work (or sector) that I want to move into?

- Shall we take the case on because we need more work in the team?

Put simply, there needs to be an additional *commercial* test applied to every case that you take on, namely:

"Is this client and this case going to add to our profit and to our cash pile in the near future?"

If the case fails the "profit and cash in the near future" test, say "No" to it, even if the answers to the above questions are all "yes". "Profit?" and "Cash?" and "Near Future?" are the deciders.

Some firms have teams or even their whole business doing work that passes the "Profit?" and "Cash?" tests but not the "Near Future?" test – long-burn Personal Injury and Clinical Negligence work, for example. I have seen firms that struggle to make this work, and I have seen others that make it work amazingly well. It can indeed work provided (1) the maximum cash is brought in and as speedily as the work-type will allow, and (2) there is enough cash in the business to pay the bills whilst the cases progress to completion. These have to be well-oiled machines to work.

But, wait a minute! Demand an exacting engagement with a new client? What about doing the first case for that new client at a low price, on the basis that "an acorn might grow into a big oak"? Forget it. That "bet" turns out favourably once every thousand times. You need to pay the bills *now* and give your staff pay rises *now*.

That "small acorn" theory is, to me, another version of the theory that drives many Private Client teams to "sell" wills cheaply. The reason they give for doing so is that "We then get the Will in our Will Bank so we get the Probate when the client dies". What, in 20 years' time?

That's new clients. Don't easily let them in. What about existing clients, though, who are already in? There are a few aspects to look at here.

First, in relation to existing clients, to me these are the "main event" when it comes to law firm growth of the right kind in the right way. Law firms spend an awful lot of money trying to win new clients. Of course, Personal Injury teams always need new clients and Conveyancing teams always need new clients. In fuller-service law firms, though, there is usually constant, costly, generic marketing aimed simply at getting more and more people to call the firm.

Graphs showing high and rising "new enquiry" levels are celebrated. They are seen as a sign of the success of general and specific marketing campaigns. They are seen as a barometer of a law firm's well-being. I don't see them as that. I don't know why there is an obsession with just getting more and more new callers and clients.

Firms are typically not making the money they should out of the cases they have already got, and are not making enough of the clients they have already got, so getting more and more of them raises overheads and risk levels and doesn't necessarily lead to a growth in profit and cash in the near future, or at all. Lawyers, teams, and firms are drowning in "busyness".

As we'll see below, doing good and effective marketing, getting a call, and converting that caller into a client is absolutely no guarantee that a firm's profit and cash will increase, particularly because the first question from a new client is usually "What's your best price?"

Law firms already have more clients who have "live" files than they could ever do anything meaningful with. If you then include "clients whose matters concluded in the last 12 months" (which we could call "lapsed" clients), the number can easily be in the thousands. So, is it better to spend a lot of money and energy and time trying to get even more clients that we do nothing with, rather than nurture and cultivate the existing clients we have already got, and harvest the considerable value that sits within that client bank?

Imagine you were a new law firm, or that you were an established law firm with just 100 clients. You could look after them amazingly. You'd make them pay a Bentley price (or at least an Audi price) for the Bentley or Audi service you gave them.

Too dear? There are enough people in the world willing to pay those high prices. Have you seen how many Audis are on the road? You could thus do less, better, for far more money. You could have a relationship with each client that transcended their initial case or work-type. You could give the cases of these 100 clients all the attention those cases needed, when they needed it.

When I was a very disgruntled client of a national law firm, I was completely hacked off with the number of "one units" that an array of lawyers had spent on my file as they snatched time on it, which added up to a massive bill. I would have far preferred them to have spent an hour at a time on it. I was happy to pay for progress, not for them to be pushing paper around (and between themselves). Clients' biggest complaint is that their bills aren't big enough.

You could offer these lucky (and happy) clients all-around care (and even proactive care) but at a high price, where the clients couldn't stay in the tent if they didn't pay you quickly. Then you could bring in another 100 clients using an amazing differentiator in your marketing. That is: "Recall what it was like when you last used lawyers? We're completely different – guaranteed".

You'd now have 200 good, value-loving, and value-adding clients with whom you have a relationship and who would be "out there" as part of your sales team: "My lawyers are dear – but very, very good".

No harm in that at all.

My main premise here is that there is an awful lot of untapped value tied up in a firm's existing client base. In my book "The Perfect Legal Business", I explored in depth the way to develop existing clients into what I call 007s, instead of always focusing on trying to win new 001s (and their penchant for cheap prices). This approach was key to my law firm becoming the UK's fastest-growing law firm – 007 really is a licence to bill.

If we accept this, and we also accept the premise that Partners are in business together, with a common view of profit, and are all on the same side, surely we can do a lot better than have a group of Partners who are effectively engaged in their own individual or team businesses every day, rather than joining forces to make one unstoppable broad legal business that did less, better, for fewer clients, across more teams, for more money?

In that kind of environment, a Partner has the time to get to know clients deeply, to understand clients' wider affairs, and to marshal all the expertise that the Partner's firm has across its teams to support and promote clients' personal and business well-being. Some sectors call it Key Account Management. Law firms call it cross-selling. I call it cross-caring.

A number of forces are at work, though, that stop this from happening. For example:

- "Personal billing" is in some Partners' DNA. They cannot contemplate doing anything else

- The firm insists that Partners have high, personal billing targets

- Partners will focus on what they are measured by and rewarded for – usually their personal billing

- There is no central mechanism or toolkit to facilitate this. Busy Partners, even if they are willing, cannot do what is needed

- There can be a "My Client" culture

- Partners don't trust other Partners

- Partners want to safeguard and ringfence their client banks, lest they want to move firms

In my first book, I set out the tools and structures that we used at my firm to crack "cross-selling" – by making it cross-caring – but none of it can happen if the views of the Partners are that it is *not going to happen*, or if the pressures on them from the firm are directed at making something else happen.

Not for the last time, I am saying that for there to be Perfect Partners in a law firm, that law firm needs to create the environment and construct the stimuli to catalyse the desired Partner behaviours.

You might not believe me, but there are CEOs and Managing Partners in law firms around the world who complain about their Partners' behaviours and contributions – see the interviews later in this book, for example. But yes, Partners can change and improve – but not if the firm won't let them and doesn't encourage them to do so, or reward them for doing so.

To bring the vast change that is possible, there needs to be, well, a partnership – a partnership between the Partners and the firm, to unleash the considerable combined "nuclear" energy that sits dormant within many Partner groups.

As you find with new clients (and our A, B, C taxonomy), you will have some As, some Bs, and some Cs with existing clients. A real C should be sacked during a case if they are not paying, or they are lying, or they are blaming, or they are being horrible. Clients who are a B can stay, though the challenge and the opportunity is to nurture and cultivate them so they become an A.

Where things get trickier is where one Partner thinks a client is an A, but in the eyes of the business as a whole, they are a C. This usually manifests itself when we look at very "big" clients. These can be clients that are big in terms of their multi-million or even billion turnover, and/or big in terms of the use they make of your firm.

They might give lots of work to various teams, or just to one team, or just to one lawyer. Often, there will be a Partner who will protect such a client. They might seek to keep the client to themselves and not open the client up to the undoubted commercial opportunities that exist for other teams in the firm.

But if the client gives you lots of work, how on Earth can they be a C? Easy:

- What is the theoretical rate or price agreed with them – is it already low?

- When was the last time your prices went up? Five years ago?

- What is the actual price they pay, bearing in mind how much extra time the Partner gives them "off the clock"?

- How much WIP is written off, particularly by junior lawyers to preserve Partner billings?

- How long do they take to pay their bills?

- What free training do they ask for and get?

- What other added value do they get? Use of precedents? Secondments?

- How much time and money is spent entertaining them or sat in reviews with them?

- What "freebies" do they and their people get from other teams?

Many "A" clients would not come out of such an examination without being downgraded. The problem is that some Partners shield "their" clients from this microscope. And often, provided the top-line billing figure is high, the firm lets these things run on.

The big fear, of course, is that if we challenge the status quo, the big client will leave us. I imagine that if your service is mediocre or worse, then a price rise or a cut-back in added value would have precisely that effect.

But ask yourself this: Why is the client still with you after all these years? The answer is not "Because we're cheap". No matter how cheap you are, no big client is going to stay with you and leave their important matters with you if the expertise or service is poor.

No, they're with you because they like what you are doing for them and the way you are doing it. What's their alternative if they don't like you raising prices as you try to convert an Apparent A into an Actual A? The alternative is possibly too awful for them to contemplate. It will mean them either starting all over again with a new law firm that knows nothing about them and their people or portfolio or estate, or it will mean them moving their work to another firm on their panel.

Again, that deprives them of the personal service from you that they have long enjoyed, and it might increase the volume of work being handled by the other panel firm to disruptive or even dangerous levels.

I have seen many examples in my work where Partners bit the bullet and decided that enough was enough. We need to see these situations not as us being grateful for a volume of work that we will do anything at any price to keep. Rather, we need to see them as relationships involving not one but *two* businesses, where the arrangement needs to work, year after year, for *both* businesses. You have much more bargaining power than you might think – if your service is good, that is. If it isn't, best keep your prices low.

To all Partners, I say, "Raise the bar!" Don't let existing or new clients have you and your firm's name behind them unless they fit the "quality" bill and are willing to agree good rates and to actually pay their bills quickly. Don't immediately bend over backwards to get them in or keep them in.

Firms of accountants are far better at this than law firms are. At various times in my business life, I sometimes wondered whether accountants actually wanted my business. They did, of course, but they put their own good name and their own profitability and cash needs first. They had the confidence to lay down a stiff set of rules from the outset. They had rails. They worked hard to very clearly define the retainer so that it was crystal clear what they were doing and what they were not doing for the agreed (high) price. They automatically required an exacting engagement, rather than an easy engagement, with their clients.

I'll never forget learning from one of my friends who was a Partner in a very big and highly successful (global) firm of accountants about their cash collection duties as Partners. If a client didn't pay on time, the Partners literally had to get in their car and stand in reception at the client's offices until a cheque was handed over. No cash? No service. What's the law firm version of that? Raise a bill so your monthly figures look good, and put it in your drawer.

Client service and support in a law firm is too often all about looking after the client and delivering on the client's wish list. It isn't enough about delivering on your own business's wish list. It is too much of a one-way street. If you haven't been a client desperate for a trusted lawyer to help you make a fortune or a crisis go away, you might not realise how strong a position you are in.

It seems to me, though, that law firm Partners are often not actually required to behave like business owners. They are often tasked with (and rewarded for) working *in* the business – that is, with being exalted fee-earners with their own fee-earning targets. Or they are indeed tasked with working *on* the business, but they still get huge personal fee-earning targets that give them precious little time and inclination to do anything other than earn fees, and no reward for doing anything else. Where that is your main driver, you live for the day rather than for developing a client over time into a good, high-paying user of all your firm's teams.

A firm and its partnership need to take a step back and breathe, and then move forward as a partnership in a determined, focused way, where you can all do less, better, for more. It's a real chicken and egg situation, though.

Many firms might feel uncomfortable in stopping what they are doing, even for a month, as their machine relies on constantly producing bills at a certain level.

It must feel like the firm cannot take its foot off that pedal, particularly because the inefficient way in which things have been done for decades has now been so challenged by the dramatic rise in salaries and overheads and the vast outflow of cash that every law firm now witnesses every month.

But I believe that the elastic has snapped and I don't think law firms can carry on doing tonnes of work, hoping that a few kilograms of cash will in effect fall out the bottom somewhere down the line. It is time to maximise cash returns on the life-changing, wealth-creating expertise that is being delivered to clients.

And it's getting harder to do even the current "day job" because it feels like there is constant and increasing interference from outside. But, as the saying goes, "rules is rules". It's time, therefore, to look at the third leg of the stool, and Partners' responsibilities in this area, too.

Compliance with internal and external rules needs to form part of the set of rails we are constructing so that the compliance leg of the stool remains strong.

CHAPTER 10

COMPLIANCE

Risk and Compliance is the third leg of the stool that we need Partners to design and protect rails to keep strong. Doing so will ensure the sustained and safe growth of their firm.

Risk is everywhere – risk that can dim the lights, make the lights flicker, or put the lights out permanently.

If we start at the shallow end of the "Risk" pool, we run the risk of doing work for clients and not getting paid for it, or the risk of being left holding the baby in relation to some hefty counsel's fees or other disbursements. Moving down the pool towards the deep end, we come to the risk of having unhappy and complaining clients – and the risk of having to write WIP or bills off.

The gradient of the pool gets very steep after that, though. There is the risk of internal Partner behaviours breaching discrimination law, SRA regulations, and internal policies. There is the risk of key lawyers leaving, and of key Business Support professionals leaving. There is the risk of clients using your firm and its bank account for nefarious purposes, the risk of reputational damage as a result of Partner behaviours in the office or on a staff night out (and the legal press and social media seem to have an abundance of such stories at the moment), the risk of Professional Indemnity claims by clients that might prejudice your PII renewal position, and the risk of cyber attacks that can (absent a huge pay-out to the perpetrators) hole you below the water line. The list goes on. Law is a risky business!

In a law firm, there is typically a huge effort and apparatus constantly at work trying to manage all of these risks and more. The Senior Management team and the Business Support teams lead the way on this. That apparatus includes a raft of rules and requirements – external rules that apply to a law firm and everyone in it – and consequential rules that Management imposes to ensure compliance with the external rules. There can also be other internal rules that relate to client management, file management, financial management, and lawyer performance and conduct.

Often, the effort put into implementing these rules is only beaten by the effort that is put in by lawyers (including, perhaps even particularly, by Partners) to circumvent the rules.

Business Support teams regularly complain to me that their main job is tidying up after Partners. They feel like they are fighting a losing battle – and that the very people who should be promoting and policing compliance are undermining it. In place of a proactive approach to compliance, with rules that are designed to materially lower risk levels, there are more cosmetic and cursory quarterly or half-yearly drives to get all files and checklists and documentation requirements up to date. Or there are drives in these directions ahead of the

Lexcel inspector coming in. "How do you get Partners to do what we need them to do?" Business Support teams literally scream.

I wonder what it is that gets a Partner, whose livelihood and wealth depends on a set of rules and procedures being adhered to by everyone in the business, to arrive at the view that those rules and procedures don't apply to them?

This is a million miles from the ideal situation where Partners enforce all the rules, lead by example, and ensure that everyone around them is compliant. It is like Partners behaving like non-Partners.

Why is this so? The answer, as it always is, is a mix of things. First, being hugely busy and under pressure from clients doesn't help. We all have limited headspace and time, and clients' matters will always get priority. Where the bar to client entry into the firm is not high, the inevitable result is an over-abundance of clients, all demanding a Partner's time. Partners don't know whether they are coming or going.

These rules and procedures are so vital, though, that the firm needs to do two things to help Partners arrive at a decision that the rules will be adhered to, *come what may*.

Firstly, the firm needs to make things simple. Whenever a firm needs its lawyers to embrace and adhere to a new system or rule, I recommend that you start with a very graphic image – an image of every lawyer's head being open, but those heads being full to the brim. There is literally no room for anything new.

What is therefore needed is an exercise in education, persuasion, and facilitation. Explain what the new rule is for, and make it as easy as possible to comply with. Supply a toolkit, as child-like in its simplicity as possible. This could be to clear balances on client accounts, or to deal with suspicious emails, or to ascertain sources of funds, or to deal with client ID. Remember, lawyers' heads are full to the brim already. Make it simple. Dovetail it with existing rules and systems. That shows the lawyers that Management is sympathetic to the lot of a highly-pressured lawyer. It helps to win their hearts and minds instead of alienating them with detached, uncoordinated Management and Business Support outpourings.

And, as I say, what is happening in relation to one rule needs to dovetail and synchronise with what is happening in relation to other rules. Different parts of the business throwing things at busy lawyers in an uncoordinated way will not secure the desired result.

Secondly, though, there needs to be a sanction if – despite these efforts – there is blatant disregard of rules and procedures. All too often, "nightmare" Partners (in terms of compliance and other contrary behaviours) are still celebrated because their rainmaking or their billing is good. The truth is their flair or their personal billing is unlikely to get the whole firm to thrive, but their recklessness in terms of compliance could bring the whole house down.

Some risks shouldn't need explaining, and the day-to-day management and control of them should be second nature to Partners. For example, the risk of mistakes being made on files. Junior lawyers don't have a monopoly on these, but junior lawyers are a healthy source of crises on files that need resolving and which can result in claims. This, in turn, can make the annual PII renewal more "exciting" than it needs to be.

It makes sense, therefore, that Partners should have their radar on, literally all the time, in relation to the quality of lawyers working on files in the firm. They need to watch the quality of legal advice, and the quality of service as that advice is delivered. Neither the Senior Management Team nor the Business Support team can have eyes and ears everywhere. Non-lawyer Business Support staff won't be able to smell issues on files like Partners will.

And yet, file reviews – the surefire way of understanding the strengths and weaknesses of your burgeoning lawyers – are routinely left to one side so that a Partner can use the time instead to record a few more units.

Sustained poor quality of service at any level, in any sector, is always Management's or the owners' fault. In a hotel where quality is poor because the rooms are below par or there is no service, that's not the fault of the cleaner or the waiter or waitress – it's the fault of Management and the owners. It's the same with law firms. How can Partners not be keenly interested in the quality of the law and the service being delivered across the firm?

This view might be met with a complaint from Partners that they are the billing engines of the firm and the firm cannot afford to have Partners doing more non-billable work. I often see this, and I see that there needs to be a shift (which I address later), so that the pyramids and teams *below* the Partners become the firm's billing engines.

And let me leave another thread dangling here that I will pick up later. I'm calling it (for now) "the magic ingredient". Any one Partner's disregard and recklessness in relation to risks and rules puts paid to this magic ingredient ever arising and it thus puts paid to the firm's prospects of ever heading to the stars.

I'll come back to this, but first let's look at the fourth and final leg of the stool that requires the Partners in a firm to put rails in place.

CHAPTER 11

CASH

The fourth and final leg of the stool that requires rails – and this leg needs to get stronger and stronger every year – is the 'Cash' leg. I don't mean the Billing leg, or the Turnover leg, or the Profit leg. Or even the "money" leg. I mean very specifically the *Cash* leg.

Let's look at how a legal business works. I mean, how it really works. And I'm going to labour some of this. I'd heard it all a dozen times, but it still didn't sink in in the way that it now has.

Some of what follows overlaps with parts of my other books, but we need it here, too, alongside all the other "Partner" areas that we will focus on. If you already know the stuff I'm about to discuss, you are in a small minority, so I make no apology if I am teaching some of you to suck eggs.

It's far better for us all to look at this afresh and either learn about, or be reminded of, the basics. They never go away, and even in the bizarre, fast-changing world we operate in, they are still the very things (and the only things) that build the foundations from which great things can be launched.

Not only do all Partners need to understand all of this, they also need to be able to educate others on it. If they can't compellingly explain it to others, how are they going to get wider buy-in? Partners are in business. They need to understand business.

So, how does a legal business work? One thing's for sure: it doesn't work in the way that it's often presented to the internal world in a law firm. And another thing's for sure – it definitely doesn't work in the way that it's always presented to the outside business world or to the legal community or to the business press. And it doesn't work in the way that things are presented to, and published by, the annual legal sector directories like Chambers and Legal 500. Nor does it work in the way you'd think by reading the annual "turnover tables" and law firms' own press releases about their growth figures.

The truth is that there is ample space for hot air when it comes to talking about how business is going at a law firm, but when you're sitting in the hot seat – believe me – *literally only one thing matters.* Cash.

Imagine an old-fashioned bath. You are looking at a law firm. When the water in the bath (the cash) runs out, it's game over. There are no taps on this bath – it is not connected to the mains. Of course it isn't, there's no automatic flow of cash into a law firm. There is, though, a gaping plughole but no plug to go in it.

Picture the scenario. Water (or cash) literally flows out of the law firm all day, every day, with the constant threat that the water in the bath will empty.

If a law firm's water position is looking precarious, it can always borrow a few bucket-loads from its bank –

their water is called an overdraft. They not only take some of that back anyway (i.e., they charge you interest) but they can also ask for it all back at any time and without notice.

There are usually lots of buckets full of water on the floor around the bath – we can call that Work In Progress, or work that's been done for clients that hasn't been billed yet. Every now and again, a big bucket gets kicked over – "They're a good client, so that was a freebie", or "It's taken me so long to do that job that we can't bill them for my time". Or only half the bucket gets poured into the bath because the fees are being discounted.

As I say, the water is constantly draining out of the large plughole in the bath. That's when the going is good. Then something bad invariably comes along. That could be a month where rent or IT licence fees or payment for practising certificates is due, or – a big one – Professional Indemnity Insurance has to be paid for. Those things are all like huge, additional holes being drilled in the bath.

But there is something you come to fear far more than those quarterly or annual pinch points. It is the monthly payday.

On the 28th of every month or so, the plughole quadruples in size. "Making payday" is a real challenge for businesses of all types around the world, and few business sectors have got the salary bill that law firms have. From the 29th, you become obsessed with whether there is going to be enough water in the bath for the next 28th.

No problem though – our lawyers are doing bills. That should fix things? Sorry. No. It can be quite the opposite if there is VAT or some other sales tax in your jurisdiction.

If there is, then contrary to what many people think, when they are raised, bills are *not* water in the bath. Actually, they are literally new holes being drilled in the bath. Every time you raise a bill, you commit your firm to paying the VAT on the bill to the government. That's 20% of the fees that are included in the bill. Once that bill is raised, the VAT contained is ordinarily due to be paid by most law firms that quarter, regardless of whether the client has paid the bill. The more bills you raise, the more VAT is due from the firm.

Where should that VAT come from? Obviously, the common-sense, natural expectation is that – as it's on the bill to the client – it should come from the clients' timely payment of that bill. In practice, where does it very often come from? Can you hear that drilling sound? The VAT all too often comes from the firm itself, out of its own limited cash resources, because the bill doesn't get paid as it should by the client.

Raising bills can thus empty your bath rather than fill it. It's insanity that lawyers, teams, and law firms can celebrate great billing months and years, where they – rather than the clients – are in fact cash-starved because they are effectively funding growth in the clients' personal or business wealth, as well as paying the very VAT that the services to the client have generated!

All the while, as well as having benefited from your top-notch legal expertise, the client – if they are a business – is using your invoice to reduce the tax they pay on their own profit and is using your invoice to reduce any VAT that they have to pay themselves that VAT quarter. It can be win, win, win for clients and pain, pain, and more pain for law firms.

As you can see, sustainable business success is about far more than the things law firms widely boast about, such as billing, turnover, "growth", awards, and so on. It's all about cash.

To help drive this concept home, we're going to start by looking at not one but three things – billing (or turnover), profit, and cash. Many people think they're the same thing. That's a deadly mistake to make. I know. I won't get fooled again.

First – billing and turnover? That's easy. In its simplest form, it's the total value of the bills that a law firm raises. This is also known as "the top line".

Next, let's look at "profit". This is not as simple as you might think, even if we ignore the outlandish way that a law firm's profit can be increased by work they haven't even billed yet.

If you sell Coke, it's easy. Assume you buy it at 40p (that's called your Direct Cost) and you sell it at £1 (that's called your billing or your turnover or your "top line"). Your profit (or rather, what's called your *Gross* Profit at this stage) is 60p.

Of course, knowing that 60p is left over for the business on the sale of every bottle of Coke is important information to have. More usually, though, the business world doesn't look at it in these *monetary* terms. Instead, it looks at how *efficient* the business is at making a profit when it sells what it sells. It does this by working out how much of the sale price is left over after the purchase price is deducted, *as a percentage*. A good business wants the highest possible amount (that is, the highest possible percentage) left over in this way.

In the above Coke example, the business sold the Coke for £1 but had to pay out 40p to buy the Coke. That means that 60% of the sale price is left over for the business when it sells a Coke. We call this percentage of the sale price that is left over the Gross Margin, and as you will see, it is the fundamental measure and driver of a law firm's business.

"Business", in general, is obsessed with Gross Margin. If a business has got a lot of money left over after it has sold what it bought to sell – i.e., it's a high margin business – that is obviously celebrated and valued. For example, top of the pile when it comes to having a great Gross Margin (where what is being sold by a business costs peanuts to acquire but it sells at a high price) is software. Once 'design and build' costs are covered, it costs nothing to run off another copy of the software and Microsoft, for example, can then command a high price for their system. And because they're in a good bargaining position, it's a great cash business, too. No pay, no licence.

So, Gross Margin is crucial, and yet I bet many of you have never heard it mentioned. We're more of a profession, aren't we, than a business? Not any more.

Moving to the next stage in the operation of any business, in the Coke business that we are talking about, that 60p of Gross Profit doesn't just go into the business owner's pocket. Oh no – there are other bills to pay! That 60p instead drops down into the next trough. As I say, how much of the billing drops into that next trough is the fundamental measure of the viability and success of a business. If you aren't making good money at Gross Profit level, everything else is doomed. I'll come back to this later.

To repeat, the business owner here doesn't walk away with that 60p Gross Profit in their pocket. Rather, it drops down into the next trough where there are always plenty of snouts waiting to get stuck into it. What then eats away at that Gross Profit of 60p is your "middle line", or the other costs that are needed to enable the business to operate. We could call them Indirect Costs, but more usually they are called Overheads. So you have your Turnover, less your Direct Costs, leaving you with your Gross Profit, but you then have to pay your Overheads out of that Gross Profit.

What exactly are Overheads? In this example, there might be the cost of the electricity to keep the cans cold. Or the cost of running a van to move the stock around. Or the cost to rent a storage unit to keep all the cans in. All those Overheads obviously have to be paid, and it stands to reason that they can only be paid out of the Gross Profit you earned on your sales. If you didn't sell the Coke at all – if business was slow – or you didn't sell the Coke for much more than you paid for it, there wouldn't be enough Gross Profit to pay these Overheads.

Once you've paid the Overheads out of the Gross Profit, you are left with your Net Profit (your "bottom line"). Only *now* can the owner (that's the Equity

Partners in a law firm) look in the till and think "At last – some money for me".

In a law firm, the exact same principles apply, just with several absolutely monumental differences. The billings in our game are much higher, but so too are the Direct Costs, and so too are the subsequent Overheads.

This all immediately undermines all law firms' boasts around growth in their "top line" or turnover, when you think that – sadly – they can't keep everything that they bill because of Direct Costs (and not the Coke we had to buy for 40p in the example above).

No – the Direct Costs in law firms are the absolutely gigantic, frightening and ever-increasing salaries that law firms have to pay their lawyers to do the thing (i.e., the law) that they are selling.

In a law firm, "Team Billings" minus "Team Salaries" gives you your team's Gross Profit. A legal team's Gross Profit is what is left over (though it's only on paper at this stage) from the team's billing after the team that did the billing have been paid. Just like in the Coke example. That Gross Profit is again in £.

As with the Coke example, we can work out how efficient a legal team is at making profit (i.e., we can work out the team's Gross Margin), by looking at the *percentage* of the team's billing that is *left over* after the team has been paid. The higher the percentage, the more of a team's billings are left over after the team has been paid. Or, to put it another way, the better the team are at generating profit. That is a key measure of how good a legal business (or part of a legal business) is.

Can I add in one complication here? The salaries I am talking about are the salaries that are paid to lawyers who are employees of the firm, including Salaried Partners. You weigh up their total billings against their total salaries to see how efficient the team is at making a profit. However, if the team has an Equity Partner in the team, an Equity Partner is an employer, not an employee. They don't get paid a salary.

An Equity Partner only gets any money if there's any money left in the till after the Direct Costs and the Overheads have been paid. They do billing, though, which means that a team could get that billing but with no associated salary cost. That would give the team an artificially high Gross Profit and Gross Margin, because lots of billing would now be left over after the low team salary bill has been deducted. What you need to do to avoid this happening – and to make sure all teams are treated the same – is to add a *notional* salary for each Equity Partner in that team to the team's salary bill. That could be the salary of a typical Salaried Partner in that area of law and that area of the country.

Carrying on with our law firm example, the bit of each team's billing that is left over after the teams' salaries have been paid (i.e., the team's Gross Profit) then goes into the next trough, exactly as it did in the Coke example.

That pot is then used to pay the law firm's Overheads – the electricity or the van in the above example. Except, in the case of a law firm, it's an awful lot more than these. It's rent, rates, IT costs, Business Support staff, Practising Certificates, Knowledge Management products and precedents, accountants' fees, marketing costs, rates, gas, electricity, and Professional Indemnity Insurance. The list is endless, and the sums are huge.

When you've sat in the hot seat as I did for nearly ten years, this stuff can frankly make you ill. And every year, it all goes up. It can go up at a shocking pace and without warning.

The amount needed to be left over after team salaries have been paid (i.e., the teams' Gross Profit) literally and simply needs to go up every year because the cost of Overheads goes up every year. But the team salaries – which are the first thing to be paid out of a team's billings – also go up every year themselves at pay rise time, so you can see the double pressure here to get team billing levels up as much as possible. They simply have to keep going up, every year, and by more than these other things are going up.

So, I hope you can see that Team Gross Profit (£) and a team's profit-making efficiency (%) is the first key to business success, *not* turnover or billings. You simply have to get the amount of a team's Gross Profit up every year, in each team, even if the teams' salary bills are going up, which they inevitably will be.

If Gross Profit doesn't go up, the pressures pass down through the system and the walls start closing in, as there won't be enough money to pay the Overheads and to leave something for the firm's owners. Good Gross Profit unlocks everything (though, as I move on to below, this is only once the team's bills have all been paid).

To increase a team's Gross Profit "leftovers" (in £) and to increase the percentage of the team's billing that is left over (i.e., their Gross Margin), if you look at how

Gross Profit and Gross Margin are calculated, you can see that there are only two things you can do:

- Get the same lawyers on the same salary bill to do more billing, or

- If there isn't enough work to enable all the lawyers to fully bill, you take some of the salary bill (i.e., some of the lawyers) out

The first of these is by far the best way to go. You can easily get the same lawyers doing more billing, and without them having to work any harder or longer.

As first steps along what I'll shortly be looking at, namely *The Money Journey*, you need to bolster and challenge your pricing positions (relying on your differentiators), you need to make sure all work is actually being done and done properly, you need to make sure every minute that is spent on client files is captured, and you need to make sure all captured time is billed.

There is more to this, though, because the increased Direct Costs in a law firm (the lawyers' salaries and their pay rises) and the increased Overheads, all have to be paid in *cash*. Even if you manage to get a team's billing and, therefore, their Gross Profit up, that is not necessarily cash – you can get a team's Gross Profit up by simply sending out more bills. Their Gross Profit may have gone up, but it might just be in terms of "bills sent out".

So the cash to pay the increased Direct Costs and to pay the higher Overheads hasn't come in yet, and – triple-whammy if VAT or a sales tax applies to you – you're having to use the firm's limited bath of cash to pay the VAT on that increased billing if those bills aren't paid quickly. Can you hear the gurgling of the last drops of water circling the plughole?

Let me show you this issue in action. If a team bills £1m in a year, and their salary bill is £470,000, then their Gross Profit (the bit of their billing left over after the team have been paid) is £530,000. That means that, on paper, 53% of their billing is left over after the team has been paid and it means, again on paper, that their Gross Margin is 53% (so not bad, though it does need to be nearer 60% these days).

What if, though, of that £1m of bills, £350,000 hasn't been paid yet? That means that whilst their Gross Profit is indeed still £530,000 in accounting terms, their *true* income generation at that point is not £1 million but is only £650,000 against the salary bill of £470,000. That gives a *real* Gross Profit now – on that £1 million of billing – of only £180,000 and a real Gross Margin on that £1m of billing of only 18%.

That is way too low to cover the team's share of the firm's Overheads – quite apart from the fact that the firm might also be in danger of having to pay VAT of £70,000 on the unpaid bills.

If the firm itself has to pay the VAT on these bills because the clients don't pay them, then the real net income generated for the firm by this team's £1m of billings is just £110,000, a long way short of what the team's £1 million of billing initially promised. On that £1m of billing, that is an effective Gross Margin of just 11%, or virtually break-even. The £1 million of billing has been virtually wiped out because £470,000 went on paying the team who did the billing, £350,000 of it hasn't yet been paid, and the firm has to pay £70,000 in VAT that the clients should have been paying. Nasty!

As well as the pay rises for a team's existing lawyers reducing a team's Gross Profit (and therefore their Gross Margin), the team's Gross Profit and its Gross Margin will also fall when you bring a new lawyer into the team, as more salary goes out from the outset, which won't be covered by the new lawyer's billing for a while. When you're busy and growing, therefore, Gross Profit may fall but will hopefully then rise as the new lawyers get into their billing stride. But that's only the "profit" dimension.

Don't forget the vital "cash" dimension when it comes to new lawyers as well as existing lawyers, though. A team's "profit" can look better as new lawyers start billing, but the firm could, in fact, be really suffering. New lawyers take cash out of the firm from their first month, and their billing – whilst adding to your profit – could take further cash out of the firm in the form of any VAT that has to be paid on their bills.

It's only when their bills get paid that a new lawyer (like an existing lawyer) shifts from being a problem for the firm to being an asset. The first aim is obviously for that new lawyer to start billing as soon as possible. But they can do all the bills they want… if those bills aren't paid, that new lawyer is killing you. You need to carefully monitor not just when they turn profitable (bills sent out) but also when they turn cash-positive (bills paid). Don't carry on recruiting blindly without knowing that previous recruits are adding to your bath rather than draining it.

You can see that in terms of "profit", the first growth we need is growth in each team's Gross Profit and Gross Margin. In terms of "cash", the first growth that we need to see is their bills being paid.

All Partners should have the following words at the forefront of their minds on every case they take on, every case that they work on, and every case that they ask others (be they peers or junior lawyers) in the firm to work on :

WHAT'S THE PROFIT, AND *WHEN'S* THE CASH?

In the same way that client service is all about PUSH & TELL (see below), the business side of things is all about WHAT & WHEN.

There is little to boast about if a team's billing increases by £100k but so do team salaries, particularly as that £100k billing may not yet have been paid and the £20k VAT on it might have to be paid by the firm in addition to the higher salary payments. And, as I have said, getting to a good position this year isn't enough. The lawyers will want pay rises next year, too, so the amount of the team's billing left over after increased team salaries have been paid goes down, unless the amount that is billed goes up by more. Every year.

I have seen law firms that were able to forecast far higher billings (i.e., a much higher top line) in the year ahead than in the previous year. But because Direct Costs and Overheads had gone up so much, both the forecasted Gross Profit and the forecasted Net Profit were actually *down* on the year before, despite their "top line" growth. The legal press seems to be full of stories of law firms boasting of higher turnover, but showing lower profits.

As a result of the way the world is going, I believe that unless and until you have the conversion on the road to Damascus that I advocate in my books, existing and aspiring law firm owners and leaders can forget all their dreams about truly giving their people great lives and opportunities. If your focus is on getting new clients or billing rather than on Gross Profit and cash, you might end up counting cash in and cash out every day, sweating as the 28th approaches.

Often, a leader tries to get their lawyers to focus on the right things, but nothing internally seems to have the desired effect, no matter how much they bark at everyone.

The inevitable result? This need for a vast and ever-increasing amount of cash doesn't go away, so the firm's leadership has no option but to look at other places where they might get the cash they need in the short term, and at other places where they might get the growth that the business needs in the medium term and the long term.

In terms of getting cash the business needs now, the firm can move to a bank that will give it a bigger overdraft, not realising of course that its flawed behaviours and structures mean that the more the firm grows by using the bank's cash to pay new salaries, etc, the quicker it is going to feel stressed.

If you are looking to get your hands on more cash because your lawyers aren't generating enough of it, you can look to the myriad other secondary lenders that are out there nowadays who will fund nearly anything you want to buy – IT hardware and software, Practising Certificates, office fit-outs, office equipment, and Tax.

Yes, tax. You can borrow money to pay the tax you have to pay on your profits, and even any VAT that is at the bottom of every bill you send out (because Heaven forbid, you don't expect your clients to pay that, do you?) You can borrow it all. Until you can't borrow it any more. Then the music stops. All this available cash allows you to mask (and allows you not to have to address) poor profit and cash behaviours.

In order to generate the needed growth in the longer terms, if the profit-making and cash-making efficiency of the law firm won't improve, as I say, the firm has to look at the other higher-cost, higher-risk routes to growth – like lateral hires, opening new offices, launching new work-types, and so on (as discussed in my first book). None of these bring returns of the size and certainty that are available if you follow the path I set out.

We need, therefore, to have the teams in a law firm performing to the maximum so that:

1. the billing hugely exceeds the teams' Direct Costs and the firm's Overheads in any one year

2. the *growth* in their billing exceeds the growth in both those costs every year

3. All bills get paid quickly

Let's look more closely at two key differences between the Coke example and a law firm. These make everything much more painful for law firms.

The first is the question of payment. In the Coke example, there is no cash "gap" – no cash from the customer, no Coke. In a law firm, clients routinely get our life-changing and wealth-creating expertise long before they have to hand over any cash.

The owner of the Coke stand doesn't hand over a fortune in Coke and then give the people who are drinking it a begging letter saying, "It'd be great if you could pay me". That's what law firms do. It's called a bill. Clients don't always respond to those begging letters in the way and with the immediacy that you want them to. Law firms need to close the cash gap – that is, to reduce the time between when a bill is raised and when it is paid.

There is a second challenge to the business health of a law firm. And that relates to *when* the bill is even raised. Often, law firms are slow at raising the bill, and are then slow at getting the bill paid. Delay on top of delay. Pain on top of pain. Who's funding the law firm while all that is going on? How many paydays have gone by since we started work on a file?

If you rise above a case you are dealing with for a client, you can see that all the firm's Direct Costs are being paid – that is, the lawyer's salary – while the case is being worked on, by the firm, while the client is benefiting from the lawyer's expertise. But surveys show that typically, across the legal sector, it is only after an astonishing, jaw-dropping *five months* after work has started on a case that any cash comes in. That's five paydays! That constantly leaves very little water in the bath. This is the great "lock-up" challenge that law firms face, and it underlines the need for a sharp move away from a pedestrian approach to converting expertise into cash. We need to ask "WHAT'S THE PROFIT?", but also "WHEN'S THE CASH?"

Over the years, despite the inefficiencies hard-wired into lawyer and team pricing and billing practices (let alone into their cash-collection behaviours), there was always enough Gross Profit left over on paper at a year-end after the lawyers in the teams had been paid to cover the then reasonable Overheads and for there still to be some left over as Net Profit (again, on paper) for the owners of the firm, the Equity Partners.

And enough of that Net Profit had been billed and turned into cash by year-end so that, when you used the overdraft that the bank allowed you to use, the owners could actually get some cash out of the business each year to make all the risk and all the pressure worthwhile.

Typically, the owners wouldn't (often because they couldn't) take all the profit out of the business in cash. They often didn't want to – they were happy to leave undrawn profits in the business, earning a good rate of interest from the firm, and there'd be a nice pot of money to pay out when the Partner retired.

This lack of pressing to get all the profit out in cash meant that everything worked. Lazy and inefficient profit, billing, and cash behaviours could be accommodated by the business and its Partners.

But things have changed. Everything has changed. Direct Costs (lawyer salaries) are now much, much higher, so that less of a team's billing is left over to go into the next pot to pay the Overheads, and those Overheads are now much greater in number and much greater in size. And they all have to be paid in cash. Law firm billing and, therefore, law firm profit have lost ground in relation to the costs needed to run a firm, and the age-old casualness or even recklessness about when bills are raised (and whether bills were paid or not) is now an existential threat.

I believe the elastic has snapped and that unless firms accept that they are not glorious success stories just because turnover or headcount or Partner numbers or office numbers or awards are rising, and unless they recalibrate their profit and cash generation priorities and behaviours, I expect to see even very successful law firms running in an out-of-breath fashion. That's a dangerous place to be. If a law firm isn't moving forwards, it's moving backwards as it will not be able to afford to keep increasing the rewards that its good people want and expect every year.

I genuinely believe that unless law firms go for TLI and shoot for the stars (by embarking on what I call "The Money Journey"), incessantly choppy waters will limit the freedom of even great law firms to choose their own destiny. It all genuinely frustrates me because I see how easy it is to change, and to change everything, quickly. Law firms just need to examine themselves and listen. It's not a sign of weakness. Taking external advice and taking action to make yourself a business that matches your standing as a law firm is something to be proud of.

You've seen that I like using metaphors to demonstrate the points I'm making. So here goes:

- If a law firm listened to all of this, it would see that – in old parlance – it's not about the beautifully-balanced stereo record player and the shiny amplifier and the graphic equaliser or the speakers or even the gold-plated cables that connect the sound system together. It's all for nothing if the needle on the record is bent

- It's not about what the car looks like or the engine size or the leather seats or the carbon fibre body or the go-faster stripes or the huge wing on the back of the car. If the tyres are bald, there's not going to be the traction you need to translate potential into progress.

You can achieve what is necessary by going on what I call The Money Journey. This comprises many of the key rails that Partners need to get their firm onto, and which the Partners then need (individually and collectively) to drive the firm along.

CHAPTER 12

THE MONEY JOURNEY

What I'm about to set out can be easily and quickly achieved. Really. In even very large law firms, it is amazing how quickly significant change can be procured so that you have everyone rowing in the right direction.

When you get to the end of this book, having looked at the rails that you need to have in place, put them into the framework of a typical Partners meeting. The necessary change isn't going to happen, is it? That's why I arrived at the view (in my second book) that the way law firms secure change has itself to change.

If the Partners *can* galvanise and come together as a unified group, then many of the steps on The Money Journey can easily be taken. If they galvanise *and* they have an internal or external unifying catalyst or catalyser, then much more than the steps in this chapter are realisable – the treasure spread throughout this book can be yours.

Partners and Managing Partners and Business Support heads frequently say to me, "I don't know how you've done all that, let alone so quickly".

Lawyers – even the very top lawyers in the country – don't hesitate to listen to legal counsel even in their own area of brilliance. And yet when it comes to business and business growth, a subject on which lawyers have usually had no meaningful training at all, the thought of listening to an outside expert (who has seen hundreds of law firms when Partners themselves have usually only seen one or two) is anathema.

It's frankly ridiculous.

The rest of the business world (which doesn't have access to the soft overdraft facilities that have always been available to law firms) has always had to (and has wanted to) seek external input to secure high business performance, and has done so with great effect. Things can happen when you involve an outside expert and facilitator that don't happen when you don't.

The people who are available to law firms in this way range from those that help you make a bit more money, to those who change destinies. I'm very much in the latter camp. Of course, "money" is a part of that.

And when you talk about "money" in the context of a law firm, to my mind the discussion has to start by talking about money at the "team" level – that's where a law firm's "money" comes from.

Looking at "money" on a team-by-team basis, ask this question: Could the business and performance of a team or teams in this firm improve? Let's ask some blunt questions to give us an answer:

Is the team sufficiently *profitable*?

You have to look at this in two ways. First, as we looked at, what percentage of the team's billing is left over after the team doing the billing has been paid?

That is, what is the team's Gross *Margin*? If it's a high percentage (60%+), there's no need to change anything. Second, though, in £ terms, what is the Gross *Profit* of the team after the team have been paid? If there is a good Gross *Profit* (i.e., there is a lot of £ left over out of a team's billings once the team itself has been paid), then obviously that is a good thing.

You can have a team with a low Gross *Margin* (e.g., "only 25% of the team's billings are left over after the team have been paid") but a high Gross *Profit* in £ – that is, because it is a huge team, there is still an awful lot of actual money in £ left over after the team have been paid.

You can have this situation when you look at a bulk, low-price conveyancing team, for example, which bills £4m and where the team salaries are £3m. As you can see, this is a low Gross Margin (just 25%), but it still gives you a Gross Profit of £1m. Not to be sniffed at.

And, conversely, you can have a small team that has a high Gross Margin, but – in fact – when you look at it in £ terms, it's not actually a lot of money. For example, take a one-lawyer team that bills £100,000, where the lawyer is paid £40,000. That's a high Gross Margin (60%), but in £ terms it's a Gross Profit of just £60,000. That won't make a meaningful difference to a law firm of any size.

So, we can't always take a team's Gross Margin as an indicator that the firm is doing well. To see if a team is *meaningfully* profitable, you have to look at both dimensions – Gross Profit (£) and Gross Margin (%).

If the lawyers in the team are expensive but the prices they charge are low, then that is "low margin" work.

Some work might be price-sensitive – e.g., conveyancing prices in certain towns. The quest must always be to increase the margins here by increasing prices and by charging extra for anything that falls outside a carefully-crafted retainer, as the only other option to give a low-margin team the growth it needs every year is to increase the volumes of the low-margin work that the team does. That has all sorts of hidden costs and risks.

Although the team's Gross Profit in £ is what ultimately counts, looking at the team's Gross Margin percentage is a really good way to see how a team is doing. It gives an easy indicator (or speedometer) that you can work with to get a team to happily and positively move towards maximum efficiency in profit-generation terms.

And we can add some science here. As a general guide, if a law firm has teams whose Gross Margins are languishing at 50% or below, it will struggle to have enough Gross Profit left over after the teams have been paid to pay the Overheads and to have anything left over after that for pay rises, for investment, and for the owners of the firm. It needs to be nearer (if not over) 60%.

In response to this first question, therefore, a team may have a "profit" challenge (or rather, a profit opportunity) if it has a low Gross Profit or a low Gross Margin.

Next question…

Does the team have bills that are unpaid after a while?

If so, then whilst your Direct Costs (the team's lawyers' salaries) and the firm's Overheads have to be paid in cash, not only are you not getting the cash in to cover those, but the firm might also have to pay VAT on the team's unpaid bills out of its own cash.

In addition to having a "profit" challenge, the team may, therefore, also have a "cash" challenge. It can actually have a "cash" challenge even if it is making huge profits on paper. All you have to do to make huge profits is send lots of bills out. It's madness, isn't it?

To see the real extent of a team's cash impact, have a look at the tool I used in my firm, which we called the Team Cash Impact Statement (which I talked about in my first book). It showed in very stark terms how different teams were lifting the firm up or weighing it down, regardless of whether they were high-performing or not, profitable or not.

It is bizarre to me (although I did it myself) that instead of changing profit and cash behaviours across their teams, many law firms are happy to accommodate their teams' inefficiencies by using someone else's money – the owners' money, or the bank's money – to run the firm, instead of getting in what is due from clients. Firms need to refuse any longer to be a "credit" or "begging" business and to move towards becoming "cash" businesses.

By the way, I don't think a team's Gross Margin and Debtor Day numbers are just for Senior Management, Team Leaders, or the Partners in a team. I think they should be made known to (and should be owned by) absolutely everyone in a team. They are a key indicator of how their team is doing. They give away no information of a sensitive or confidential nature in teams of any size, and they can help to galvanise individual and team action.

To see if improvement in a team's performance is possible or in fact needed, those are the first two questions to ask of any team in a law firm.

It follows that if a team's Gross Margin is up at 60%+ and its Debtor Days are below 30, then – since it is a high-margin business and a cash business – you can put this book away. If not, read on, as you will benefit by going on The Money Journey.

Here are the steps that make up The Money Journey that every team and firm should go on. It includes some of the key rails we need to have in place.

If you and your Partners are not doing these things, stop! Literally, there's no point doing anything else. What follows is a chronological look at each step of the journey that every team and firm should go on:

1. Get the phone to ring

Get your phone to ring by making your law firm stand out from the crowd. But what are your differentiators? Most law firms have the same "differentiators". So they're not really differentiators. If you haven't got a differentiator, you'll need to go cheap and compete on price. That's the only real differentiator open to you if you have nothing else powerful to say. And having differentiators that are "hot air" isn't good enough – for example, words on a website that mean nothing in reality. We inhabit an industry where hot air is produced on an industrial scale.

We don't want hot air – we want concrete. We need a differentiator that is meaningful and that you deliver on – every time. I help firms to design new differentiators and to hone their existing ones, and – crucially – to then deliver on them, all the time. As a profession, we seem to think we can get away with nice but vacuous words.

The main differentiators that I help law firms to build are around delivering a guaranteed, consistent client experience when they use a firm and around truly caring for clients – in building relationships rather than those firms just being involved in transactions with their clients. Despite the long wish-list I believe clients can have of their lawyers, I feel that quality clients quite reasonably only want two things when all is said and done.

First, they want to effectively be your only client. You can make them feel like that if you (and your team and your firm, as it takes all of you) constantly push their case, and constantly tell them where their case is up to and what comes next.

This simple, almost child-like concept of "Push & Tell" has really caught on since my first book, where I explained how this was what we had built at my firm.

But building something that genuinely works here takes concrete rather than hot air. The kind of differentiator I am talking about involves everyone in the firm in its design and its delivery.

There are numerous law firms that carry promises to their clients on their websites, and I have even seen versions of the kind of Service Pledge that I have engineered with various law firms, copied and pasted onto law firms' websites. I have ascertained that in those firms, the staff don't know what their firm's promise to clients is, and don't even know that it is on their website. It's far from being in the firm's DNA.

When I say "everyone" needs to be involved in the design of the differentiator, I mean "everyone, including Partners", of course. Yes, they too need to do what is necessary if a firm is to design and then deliver on the differentiator. They need to do it individually. And if they all do it individually, so that they are doing it collectively, then it is "magic ingredient" time.

Once you have a differentiator that you are proud of, and that you always deliver on, then you will have that rarest of things in the legal sector – a promise – better known as a brand. A "brand" is not a name or a logo, it's a promise that you deliver on. A brand in a law firm would be a great generator of both profit and pride.

2. Next, set a good core price

At my firm, we genuinely built a brand – we delivered on our promise of delivering "A Great Service – Every Lawyer, Every Time". What I failed to do, though, was ensure that we charged a good price for that. We delivered Bentley Law but only charged a Ford price. We didn't raise the bar in all the ways that we should have.

So, as the next step on The Money Journey, the phone has rung because of your differentiators, but we need to raise the bar and be more exacting in the ways we looked at earlier, before we take on a new client and a new matter.

Let's have pride in the guaranteed legal and service excellence that is our concrete differentiator, but let's have real pride in how we command a good price for that excellence, too.

Let's be proud of how we operate as a business, as well as being proud of how we operate as lawyers. The first step towards achieving this is to set a good core price. That could be based on an hourly rate, or on a fixed price.

Much is being made across legal sector social media about the end of time recording and the end of the hourly rate being upon us. Whilst I see efforts to unbundle usually time-charged work, I simply don't see the decline of the hourly rate and time-charge pricing in practice, and I don't see it coming any time soon. Some teams have, of course, never had it and don't have it now – corporate and property transactions (commercial and residential), for example, have long been based on fixed prices.

If it is hourly-rate work, the client will want to know what your hourly rate is and what the overall cost estimate is. The former is easier to explain than the latter, and it is understandable that a client will seize on your hourly rate and compare it to that of other firms they have spoken to. The temptation might be for the lawyer to say, "We'll do it for the same" or "We can do it cheaper than that" in order to secure the instruction. If you've got nothing powerful to say, then you might just have to do that to land the job. If you have got something powerful to say, however, about the legal and service excellence they'll get from you and your firm, and the value you'll add to their personal or business life, then explain all of that and – after you've done so – explain what you charge for your personal legal magic. Have pride in pricing and raise the bar. If they want cheap, say goodbye to them.

In fixed price work, the challenge is to get the core fixed price up (by having confidence in your legal and service differentiators and, as above, by being able to articulate them and the value you deliver, in a concrete way, before you give the number). Also, you must carefully define the retainer so that mission creep is avoided and the firm gets paid for absolutely everything it does for a client.

One trend or hope is for lawyers, in both work that is currently time-charged and currently charged by way of a fixed price, to try to better reflect *the value* of the job to the client in the price that they quote. My experience was always that far from welcoming "value pricing", clients actually struggled with it.

Take a Corporate client's terms and conditions, for example. The company's entire business depends on these being relevant, up-to-date, tailored, and watertight. In "value" terms, therefore, terms and conditions are huge. Try telling a company that the price for drafting them is therefore very high!

Whilst the chargeable hour's future is not universal – it has long since gone in some teams – I do not believe it will end in many areas of contentious work. It is perfectly open to law firms to offer clients an alternative – indeed, to offer them a range of options –

but I believe the penchant for very many clients will be a willingness to take the rough with the smooth that comes with time-based billing.

I believe that whilst clients dislike paying a lot of money for the time spent by their lawyer, they dislike paying for time that hasn't been spent by their lawyer even more.

Will Artificial Intelligence change things in both time-charged work and fixed-price work, where a job that might once have taken five hours of an Associate's time will now only take a few minutes of AI's time and one hour of an Associate's finessing?

It absolutely will! But we should harness this, not run away from it.

In some ways, we have been here before in terms of new things that changed how lawyers delivered law, and in terms of how we charged for the reduced time it took to deliver that law.

Remember when typewriters were replaced with word processors, when word processors were replaced with computers, or when law libraries were replaced by the internet?

Or when letters were replaced by faxes, when faxes were replaced by emails, and when face-to-face meetings (and travel to them) were replaced with online meetings?

As a profession and a business sector, we absorbed all these things. They all did two things – they challenged and changed the way we delivered legal services, and they challenged and changed the way we made money and how we charged clients for those legal services. AI is the next chapter in this profession's evolution.

I believe that AI will hugely change and improve the ways that lawyers deliver law to their clients, and the time it takes to deliver that law. However, it will still need lawyers to be involved. If you harness it as it develops and unfolds, you can use it to strengthen your differentiators.

It will also change how law firms operate and report internally. It will improve transparency and business analysis, and it will speed up internal processes. It should be a major tool when it comes to analysing a firm's clients and their needs, and to the instigation of really effective marketing campaigns.

But will it change *who* delivers law, to the detriment of law firms? I don't see it, myself. I can see that some people or businesses who might not have been willing or financially able to use lawyers before will be able to now access legal advice and draft letters and contracts using AI, but this is a welcome increase in access to legal expertise rather than an unwelcome decrease in the number of clients who will instruct law firms. If AI-led efficiencies are reflected in service levels and prices, it could actually increase the number of people who instruct law firms.

In the way that it already is at some visionary law firms, I believe that AI is going to be extremely useful for one group of lawyers, and it will seriously damage another group.

I believe it will help lawyers, who are already successful and busy, to hugely improve service levels and to hugely improve profitability and cashflow.

With a pipeline of work to get through and a queue of clients waiting to hear from them, these busy Partners and junior lawyers can harness AI to better progress the waiting cases. Whereas it might have taken five hours to do a job with a resulting fee of say £3,000, now the job will be done in 2 hours with a resulting fee of say £1,500.

The client will be happy with speed, service, and price, and the busy lawyers can move on to the next job. For the law firm, £1,500 has come through the door far quicker than the £3,000 was ever going to. Yes, fees on that job are down, but fees billed and cash received over the year will be up, as the cash pipeline is brought forward.

Properly harnessed AI will better enable a busy law firm to boast of the differentiator I mentioned above – a guaranteed great service, every time, and at lower fees. Happy client, happy senior lawyer, happy junior lawyer, happy business.

If you are, on the other hand, a lawyer who is not busy, AI could kill your business if you try to carry on working in old ways and at the old prices. Eventually, the market will drive you out of business because clients will know that the market rate for that job will be £1,500, not the £3,000 you are quoting, and your archaic turnaround times won't get many takers.

3. Next, define and limit the retainer

This is all about the WHAT and the WHEN.

First, what is the price and what does it cover? The core price for the core job is one thing. "Price", though, needs to be elastic – even when you are giving a fixed price – so that any work needed as a result of even a slight departure from the original brief attracts extra fees.

I can't believe some lawyers still think it is okay to try to claw back extra money when a job has overrun on a fixed price or an estimate by ringing the client at the end of the job for one of those difficult chats. It has happened to me as a client, and I loathed it.

There is a different way to go about it, and far from being abhorred by it – as lawyers might expect clients to be – clients are very open to it and welcome its honesty and transparency. It's how they live their lives, and it's how they themselves do business.

There are two parts to it:

1. It starts with the retainer being very carefully defined. If you've got five hours to chop down a tree, you should spend the first four sharpening the axe. So it is here. Spend time as an individual lawyer and as a team defining what a job entails, and itemise it in detail in the retainer letter. It will be time invested that gives a good return many times over.

    The limits on what is included in the core price can relate to issues, parties, volume of evidence, the assets or properties involved, and so on. It can also relate to the date by which the job is expected to be completed. It might relate to the conduct of the other side – or indeed to the conduct of your own client.

2. As soon as the case steps outside of that definition, we are obviously in new territory. There is no need for an uncomfortable call to the client – it's clearly new territory outside the core price, so the extra charge for dealing with it will be £X. Easy. Transparent. You don't expect a second bottle of wine or a dessert in a restaurant without paying for it. What's the difference here?

   But you do have to raise it with the client immediately after it arises. I have seen this process work in action, and it works really well. Clients are not surprised by it or put off by it. It doesn't leave that bad taste in the client's mouth that the "call at the end of the case" leaves. Try it. Make yourself try it.

As well as being about the WHAT?, it is also about the WHEN? That is, WHEN will we bill the client, and WHEN will the client pay?

To close the cash gap, we need to bill quickly and/or often in every type of work, and there then has to be a short credit period within which the client has to pay the bill. Have you closed all these doors through which early cash for the business can escape?

4. Next, do the work, do it properly, and deliver on your service promise

It's all well and good boasting of your "Bentley" service and commanding a high price for it, and the client having agreed a high price in order to avail themselves of your legal and service excellence… you've now got to deliver on your promise to them. There is nothing to be gained and everything to be lost by putting that file at the back of (or under) a desk or in the electronic version of a cabinet.

We've got to do the work. And we've got to do it properly and fully and in a timely fashion, all of which are the opposite of putting the file into storage or snatching time on the file when you have to. Avoid STORE & SNATCH! It's easier said than done.

If you "store and snatch" instead of "push and tell", your promise breaks down and your differentiator turns into hot air, just like everyone else's.

Most firms don't even try. They're content with the empty words on their website. There is no firm-wide galvanising to really design (and deliver on) the great differentiator that "service" and "client experience" can be.

In truth, an individual lawyer can simply never deliver on a service pledge unless they're not busy. It's an all-team and indeed an all-firm challenge. Unless you've got little work on as a Partner, the only way a busy Partner can keep every case moving forward, all the time, is to work with other lawyers.

You can kill multiple birds with one stone here by having good vessels (junior lawyers) in place below you, and by filling those vessels with delegated tasks to keep all your cases moving.

You would expect Partners to have the biggest cases in the firm. What happens when you delegate parts of those big cases to junior lawyers is good on a range of levels:

- The stress on you is reduced – you are happy

- You keep the pressure up on the other side – you and the client are happy

- The case keeps moving forward – the client is even happier

- The junior lawyer gets exposure to far bigger cases than if they were dumped with a usual junior lawyer's caseload – they are happy

- Files in storage make no money so a moving file makes the business happy, too

- Far more money is being made than if the Partner just tried to snatch time on files instead. A pressured Partner working at high speed can turn a case that requires £10k of time into one where they just give it £5k of time.

But "delegation" isn't "dumping". It's a real skill. It's about spending time with the junior lawyer, telling them about the case and the law and the task you are assigning to them. There's a word for it, which we'll come to later. It's part of the magic ingredient.

If you, as a Partner, have a caseload that crushes you, but you are keeping hold of every task on every file because it means you'll personally have a really good year's billing (because that's what you get rewarded for), everyone is losing out – you, the firm, the lawyers around you, and the clients.

You can see that, yes, a Partner may need to change, but so too might the firm's approach to Partner reward. You will see a theme building – you can't have "Perfect

Partners" unless the firm allows them to be and encourages them to be.

5. Next step on The Money Journey, the next rail – capture every minute of the time spent by all lawyers on client files

When work is being done and done properly, all time has to be recorded. It's great for the client but awful for the business if it is not recorded. Across all Partners and lawyers in the UK, I have seen in many firms (and I have seen in wider surveys) that the average recorded hours per day is less than 4. I saw one survey recently that said the figure was as low as 3.5 per day. That's incredible. The lawyers are *doing* about 7, but are *recording* less than 4. They are lawyers all day but are only in business in the morning; they are acting as a charity in the afternoon. Lawyers are repeatedly told this, but do nothing to improve it. That number is so low it's staggering. That this carries on year after year is all the more mindboggling. To fix this, no one needs to work any harder – they just need to catch more of the work they are already doing.

Lawyers are often given chargeable hours targets, but are rewarded and promoted when they fall way short of that target, because they still manage to hit their other, billing target. What does that tell lawyers about their chargeable hours targets? It tells them that they can ignore them as there is no sanction for not recording all the time they spend on client files, because they have hit another target (one that is artificially low, and one which has frankly had its day).

This is one of the central areas where I believe that in the business of law, failure is built into the system. There is an invisible ceiling on what lawyers agree to bill each year. It is usually a bit higher than what they billed the year before (though, of course, their rates will go up so it doesn't involve any change on the part of the lawyer) and it typically cannot break the golden rule that "My billing target can't be more than 3x my salary".

That custom and that position, which defends and bakes in outrageous inefficiency, is now punishing law firms. It is holding firms – and their people – back. Lawyers now need to achieve billings way higher than these formulae allow if the rewards and increases of the past are to continue, let alone increase. All it needs is more efficiency, not more work.

Bearing in mind that no one needs to work any harder to achieve a paradigm shift in the profit that a law firm can produce, so that the rewards available for *everyone* in the firm can be materially greater, you'd think everyone in a firm could team up to build an "efficiency masterplan" where absolutely every minute spent by all lawyers in the firm on client matters was caught and converted into money. You'd be making sure no Coke at all was ever given away.

But, when all is said and done, no one can catch and record the time except the lawyers individually – this is down to the individual Partner or junior lawyer.

Own your numbers. This is a question of personal accountability. It's also a question of dual pride – pride in what you do in law, and pride in what you do in business. You're letting yourself – and everyone else in the firm – down if you are giving your passion and your expertise away to clients. There are lots of very hardworking people in law firms who can't do anything about billing levels. As a Partner, you can, and if you aren't, you are holding yourself back (which is crazy) and all of those other people in the firm too (which is downright mean). Act like the thrifty shopkeeper (see below). And don't hide – bring out your challenges, turn things around, and become a champion (a leader!) who helps others to do the same.

The firm can help lawyers to focus on this and to deliver on their duty to the firm and everyone in the business. Lawyers need to be rewarded for chargeable hours done and recorded – not for their billing.

If, despite all efforts and training, a busy lawyer is still not recording a good deal of the time they give to clients, there have to be escalating sanctions.

They are ruining it for everyone in the firm. They are literally throwing away the firm's money. The firm has attracted a case worth, say, £10k to the business, but such lawyers are reducing it to a £5k case. The firm needs to have lawyers that turn a £10k case into a £10k case.

There should be absolutely no grey areas in a firm over what time spent on files gets recorded. An email in? An email out? Talking to a colleague about a file? Have a clear policy that applies to everyone.

Have that policy built into your Terms and Conditions with your clients. Not only are you being transparent with them, but you can then underline internally that no lawyer in the firm has the right to amend the terms the firm has agreed with its clients.

We need a clear pitch for the lawyers to play on. Interruptions are the bane of a lawyer's life, so let's reduce them. Self-inflicted interruptions first – put your smartphone in an envelope and look at it once an hour. It is costing you a fortune.

Team interruptions next. Have a period (and it can be as long as you like) where there are no team admin emails, no team meetings, and no non-urgent interruptions by the rest of the team.

Going wider than that, why not get the whole firm geared up so that all non-chargeable emails and meetings and training sessions, etc., take place after 4 pm. "Admin before 4? Show it the door!" Usually, Business Support teams are doing their very best to help the firm, each fighting their own corner but possibly without coordination between themselves and without comprehending the impact of their combined communications on the firm's lawyers' productivity. The deal, however, has to be that when the wave of admin emails, etc., arrives at 4 pm, lawyers will deal with them; otherwise, things will grind to a halt

Now, you've got the work and fewer interruptions, you can get on with doing the work *and recording the time.* Except, it's not actually "time recording".

The "less than 4 hours a day" that an average lawyer records is even worse than you might have first thought, because a lot of those "4 hours" will be "units" where effectively 6 minutes was recorded, but it might only have taken 10 seconds to trigger that unit being recorded.

As I say in the time-recording workshops that form part of my "Perfect Legal Business" programme, even with all the above parts of the masterplan in place, every lawyer needs to find a system that works for them. Doing "big" jobs that are time-based in the morning, like drafting, lets you get big hours down on the system. Check where you are up to at 1 pm – 'Got all the time that you've spent so far in the day onto the system?' In the afternoon, you can switch to the "units" work where you work through your task list, your diary system, and your inbox, firing out emails and dealing with replies. You can literally pile units up, provided you catch them all.

Things vary from work-type to work-type, but in every case, it is the lawyer's responsibility to find a way that works for them that helps to catch all of their time and all of their units.

For all lawyers, though, there comes a moment in the day when it all really happens, or it all really falls apart. Let me introduce you to the thrifty Victorian shopkeeper that I use as my hero in my time-recording masterclass.

Imagine an old shop that is crazy-busy all day – customers pouring in, buying "stuff", throwing money at the shopkeeper. If the shopkeeper worked until they couldn't work any more and then just walked out, what would that look like? Chaos. The shelves would be empty. There would be produce all over the floor. The till would be spilling over with money. There'd be money on the floor, under the counter, and falling between the floorboards. That's what many lawyers' desks kind of look like at the end of a day.

Naturally, the thrifty shopkeeper doesn't operate in that way. They wouldn't last long. They'd have unhappy customers, and they'd run out of profit and cash. So, what do they do?

The first thing they do is deliberately choose to close the shop at a certain time. They turn the sign around and lock the door. *Having served customers all day, it's now time to serve the business.* All the money is gathered up from under the till and under the counter. Knowing how much produce they've sold, they keep looking until all the money is found and put in the till. Why don't we do that as lawyers?

We, too, should bring our day to a formal and certain end, and then do two things, the first of which is to make sure we have gathered in and captured all that day's time and units (that is, *our* "money").

The second thing we should do is what the shopkeeper does next. They don't just walk away thinking, "What a day! I've no idea where all the money's gone." They collect all the money and then get the shop and its shelves ready for the following day, so they are restocked and ready to go when tomorrow's crowds arrive.

Likewise, having stopped their day at some point, and having gathered in all that day's money, the lawyer should then get tomorrow's cases lined up to work on, so they hit the ground running the following morning. Needs and opportunities to delegate work to junior lawyers can be identified. If it suits the work-type in question, "time" jobs can be lined up for the morning, and the smaller "unit" jobs can be the focus of the afternoon.

Some work-types won't allow this; it can be "unit" jobs all day long. In which case, you need a system to catch every unit you spend on every file as things fly in and out of your inbox and phone. Master and harness your firm's time-recording system. Try slips of paper with handwritten notes scribbled on them at high speed – anything that works – as you are ultimately talking about your destiny and the destiny of the business here.

And all of this is aided, made possible, and encouraged by the team-wide and firm-wide clearing of the pitch so that interruptions are minimised, and by the fact that everything (including lawyer reward, progression, and sanctions) is geared around service delivery and around revenue inputs rather than around the revenue output that is a low billing target. The latter can reward inefficiency, which is just not good for the business, its Partners, and all its other people.

6. Next step on The Money Journey, and the next rail – bill all the time that has been captured

It's one thing doing a lot of work and getting a lot of time recorded on a file – say £1,412. It's another thing altogether, billing all that time.

If you billed the full £1,412, in this example, then you would have a 100% Recovery (or Realisation) rate. If you quoted a fixed price of £1,500 and you billed £1,500 when the time on the clock was only £1,412, then you'd have a Realisation rate of over 100%, which is great.

If you have £1,412 on the clock but you bill £850 because that was the fixed price you gave, or because "They're a good client who give us lots of work", or because "That's what we've always charged them", then your Realisation rate is way down.

To succeed on The Money Journey, you need to get your Realisation rate as close as you can to 100% (assuming the team in question records time). That could mean increasing the estimates and fixed prices you quote (by relying on your differentiators) so that no recorded time has to be written off, by defining the retainer and charging extra fees for extra work, or simply by stopping the extension of discounts to any client.

The problem (and therefore the opportunity) here is all the greater when you see this Realisation challenge not in isolation but as part of a Partner's wider financial behaviours.

It is not uncommon to see senior lawyers recording just 70% of a reasonable chargeable hours target of 5 a day.

It's not unusual either to see even senior lawyers have a Realisation rate in relation to the time that they have recorded, of 75%.

This means that they are billing 75% of 70% of a reasonable production day, or a mere 52% of it, or between 2 and 3 hours. They are literally only an asset to the business in the morning. If their cash collection behaviours are similarly questionable and the firm is having to pay the VAT that falls due on their unpaid bills, you can quickly see how a Partner working in these ways is more of a problem than an asset.

Each lawyer, each team, each Team Leader, and every Partner needs to understand why realisation rates are below 100% of the time recorded. No stone should be left unturned to then close the gap between recorded value and billed value – and that includes looking at sacred cows and "great" clients, as I talked about above.

7. Next – get all bills paid quickly

Even if a Partner gets all that has gone before perfect, it's all actually damaging for the business unless cash is generated. Why?

- "Price" produces "profit", not cash

- "Productivity" produces "profit", not cash

- "Time recording" generates "profit", not cash

- "Realisation" generates profit, not cash

- "Billing" generates "profit", not cash

It's all hot air. These things are useless if something extra is not produced – cash! None of these things on their own produces "cash". That's a completely separate challenge.

Many clients are understandably not keen to hand over their cash. Your business clients, for example, might be managing precarious cashflow positions where they are tightly controlling money coming in and money going out. For personal clients, any lawyer's bill – particularly when you add any VAT to it – is going to be an unusually large item of expenditure.

A fundamental strand in the DNA of "business" around the world is *cash*. Businesses "out there" are obsessed with it. We are much less so in the legal sector. "No need to worry about cash – we can use the overdraft facility our bank allows us."

Running a huge overdraft – where things can get tight come payday every month – is not unusual in the legal sector. That's insanity when the debts owed by clients are often many times the size of the overdraft.

It is also madness because the firm might be paying VAT on the unpaid bills, and the bank is charging a high interest rate on the money they are letting the law firm use. In turn, a bank can change its mind about extending the overdraft to a firm overnight. That has left many a firm high and dry.

Typically, businesses "out there" don't have the luxury of the huge overdraft facilities that are routinely extended to law firms by banks. Law firms can therefore be lazy and use someone else's cash instead of having to rely solely on the cash that their own business operation generates.

In law firm DNA, "cash" has been replaced with other things. Like "billing", for example. Or "turnover". Both are misleading and uninformative. Even "profit" in the context of a law firm is misleading. A firm could have high profit, but that profit could be in the form of unbilled WIP and unpaid bills – all of which make "profit" a load of smoke and mirrors. No, only one thing counts, and to Partners in a law firm, *only one thing should count*… cash.

On the one hand, and bizarrely, a business with no profit can keep going forever if it has access to cash.

Think Uber, or Google. Or Amazon. Or Tesla. Why do investors hungrily buy shares in these companies when most are nowhere near making a profit for years?

The answer is that the investors are backing these companies' cashflow positions – they can keep going forever because of the cash the investors have pumped into them, and cash from sales being made, and they will turn a huge profit one day. It's literally all about the cash.

On the other hand, a business with lots of profit but no cash, dies immediately.

Why doesn't cash have the same hegemony when we look at business behaviours in law firms? It absolutely should have. Law firms are no different to other businesses. In fact, they're worse because of the relatively astronomical salaries commanded by our professionals. Cash needs to be brought centre-stage by everyone in a law firm, instead of being something that the Managing Partner or CEO and the Finance Director and the Credit Control team deal with behind the scenes each month to make sure payroll can be met. This is central to the role and responsibilities of every Partner in a law firm. Cash is a key rail.

You have, therefore, to make cash and its collection the priority in all that you do. In your engagement with clients, and in every case you work on, ask every time: What's the cash angle? How can we get the maximum cash in, and how can we get cash in sooner rather than later (as it's about both the amount of cash but also the speed of getting it in). Can you get money on account?

Can you raise interim bills? Fight your corner on this. Making it easier for clients makes it more difficult for your firm.

At the very least, you should secure absolute certainty on the amount to be billed, and the timing of the raising of bills, and the time for payment of those bills. Clients are perfectly happy to let WIP on their files get older and older if their matter is not completed. Don't stand for that.

As part of your retainer (relying again on your differentiators) and as part of an exacting engagement that is beneficial to two businesses rather than just to one, set out a timeframe for interim billing and payments. It could be (and should be) every month, with money having been taken on account so that the bill can be paid and the hole in the bath caused by the bill can be repaired immediately.

In property or corporate transactions, your clients need to know that if they want your service and expertise, the whole thing has to support your business as well, not just theirs, as you work to make them rich. They cannot expect you to work without being paid for long periods of time. Who on earth do they think is paying to keep the law firm going? Someone else?

Again, don't underestimate your bargaining power here. You don't have to just get what you are given by clients. Of course a client would like a corporate or property transaction to only be billed on completion. That works for them, but it doesn't work for you. What if you insist on interim bills? What's the client's choice – go to a lawyer that doesn't know them or who wasn't their first choice?

All too often, clients can only see things from one perspective – theirs. It takes courage and indeed training and practice to, for example, educate business clients so they see that the arrangement has to work for two businesses, not just one.

When it comes to private-paying work, what a firm can do here (in terms of bringing in maximum cash with the minimum delay) depends on the work-type in question. We can divide these work-types into three:

- Fast-burn – for example, Commercial Litigation/DR, Residential Conveyancing, Private Client, Employment – where monthly billing is possible or the transaction or advice completes quickly (within weeks)

- Medium-burn – For example, Commercial Property, Corporate – where transactions complete within months

- Slow-burn – For example, serious Personal Injury cases, and Clinical Negligence cases – where it can take years before any cash is generated for the firm

If you look at these work-types through the "cash" microscope, you can see that if you only do slow-burn work, a lot of cash is needed from other sources to run and grow a firm whilst the slow-burn cases proceed towards conclusion.

Often, you see law firms do a mix of all these work-types, so that the fast-burn work generates the day-to-day cash that the firm needs (assuming the bills get paid) and the fees generated by the medium-burn and slow-burn work (which are usually receivable in cash when a case concludes) is the icing on the cake.

When a firm has not got its "cash" house in order, then even though the fast-burn work is producing *bills* quickly, it might not be producing the cash that is needed to keep the lights burning brightly (and in VAT terms, it might be draining the firm of cash).

Decisions might have been made in some firms in recent years to stop doing slow-burn work, because the firm was having cash pressures. Whilst the slow-burn nature of the work might have been identified as the issue, profit and cash issues may have existed elsewhere in the firm, which made things feel tight and which initiated a search for immediate and apparent improvements that could be made. Thus, slow-burn teams were obviously in the crosshairs.

8. Get all the work your good clients have got, and extend maximum care to them

If you have heard me speak at legal sector events or on legal sector webinars, or you have read my other books, you will know the value I see in a law firm's existing client base.

As with everything else I talk about, it's not new, it's not my own idea, and it's not rocket science, though I do believe I have done more good work here than many other law firms and consultants have. The firm I led became built around this priority.

"Business" as a whole is acutely tuned into this concept – they call it "increasing spend per head". Its aim is to generate more revenue from existing customers without the usual marketing cost or customer-acquisition cost attached, so it is more profitable than money coming in from brand-new clients that they've had to market to. It is also less price-sensitive revenue, making it yet more profitable, as well as it being work that is more easily and cheaply attainable.

If you look around you, everyone is at it. Everyone that you do some business with is trying to get more of your wallet:

- Petrol stations now have supermarkets and takeaways and off-licences inside

- Your bank wants you to borrow more and more money for cars or extensions

- Your motor insurers are selling Home & Contents policies to you

- Dentists are increasingly offering "hearing" diagnostic services and hearing aids

Members of the public and businesses are subject to relentless upselling and cross-selling like this. *Except when they use a lawyer.*

When they use a law firm, they typically use one lawyer in a firm and just in one area of law. There are often plenty of other lawyers in a firm that could be of value to the client, but the twain never meet.

This topic is a well-trodden path in my other books, where I demonstrate how we achieved great things on this front in my firm by cross-caring rather than cross-selling, and by:

- Having central ownership of all clients

- Having no "my client" behaviours anywhere in the firm

- By having our marketing focus on developing relationships with existing clients rather than on always winning new clients

- By having trust between all our lawyers across all our teams – there was an internal service commitment as well as the external one

- By the delivery from all our teams on our promise that we would deliver a great service – every lawyer, every time

Many suppliers manage to increase spend per head amongst their customer and client base by selling them things they don't actually need. That's out-and-out, hard-core sales tactics. It's like when I went to Costco to buy some bulk household cleaning stuff and I came away with a life-size rubber torso punchbag that I could use for boxing training (it was on offer). I never used it once.

When it comes to law firms, that approach is not what I advocate, and it is not what we did. Instead, We were engaged in an incredibly valuable, caring approach to our existing clients, which ensured that they got great legal services when needed (and even ahead of their needs, so that their future traumas and legal expenses were reduced; see below). The approach I am advocating can be a real source of pride within a law firm, not something that lawyers need fear.

Let's have a look at a law firm's existing clients. Of course, I am assuming here that the law firm in question offers a range of services – the opportunities here to extend care to clients are much more limited in niche firms.

In my view, law firms typically have too many "live" or recent and lapsed clients to do anything constructive with them. I have great hopes that AI will help to change this, so that what is possible in terms of client care will transcend even what I advocate.

Subject (of course) to the clients themselves and the work-types you offer, a large number of a firm's current and lapsed clients will need more of your legal services than they initially approached you for. Team A could do very well out of the clients of Team B, and so on. A law firm's marketing and Business Development focus should be here, rather than being directed at trying to get new clients (whose first question will always be "What's your best price?"). Law firms constantly look out the window for the business growth they want and need. Close the curtains and the shutters, I say, and look inwards.

Getting more work from your existing clients is a key part of "The Money Journey":

- There is plenty of work available

- It comes at nil acquisition cost

- Conversion rates are higher as the clients have already experienced your service levels

- The clients are less concerned about price – they just want the quality they are used to

- You don't need to wait for anything to hit the fan. There are aspects that you can help clients with now – they just don't know it yet

Why wouldn't you focus on this dimension? Why would you instead focus on uncertain, expensive, low-success initiatives, where the prize is frequently a client wanting a cheap service?

Partners are key to facilitating this game-changing approach to client care (which is also extremely good for business). The Partners can move a firm from being one where particular lawyers care about particular parts of a client's life or business, to being one where the whole ethos of the firm is "care", in a holistic way – where clients' wider well-being is put ahead of an individual Partner's or a particular team's billing. Partners can help the firm to do this, or they can prevent the firm from doing it.

9. The final part of The Money Journey, extend care to your good clients *proactively*

If we really are in the "care" game – and I believe we are – then we can do a lot more for our clients than care for the case that a client brings to us.

We can look under the bonnet with the client and see whether they are exposed right now (in their personal lives, business lives, or both) to any risks that we might be able to help them to reduce or extinguish – now, before anything explodes. There are a host of ways that lawyers can proactively help a client.

As I have regaled elsewhere, we did this in my firm by helping clients to get onto personal and/or business "Platforms".

These were proactive initiatives by us that helped clients really get all their personal and business affairs in order, and to thus actually *reduce* their legal spend over the coming years. We went a lot further than what I see in most law firms, where (for example) effort in this valuable area is limited to a letter, relating to a house sale, suggesting that a client should have a will in place.

If all the lawyers and Partners in a firm were driven by a desire to care for clients rather than to bill them, the result would be amazing for clients and amazing for the business. It has to be led by the Partners, though. And they ought not fear that this is *selling*. It isn't – it's *caring*. It can have a dramatic impact on what unfolds for a client. Isn't that what we're here for?

In this vein, the fast-food company McDonald's famously generated billions of dollars in revenue out of *its* existing customers by training its staff to ask one simple question of them all, namely, "Would you like fries with that?" That is absolutely *not* what we are talking about here. We are not just talking about, as an example, a Commercial Property Partner saying to their client, "We do Employment law too".

What I am saying is that the Commercial Property Partner should have the mindset of being curious about who is doing the client's Employment work. They should wonder whether the client is getting a great service, every time, from those other lawyers, and whether the client has everything in place – in Employment law terms – to make sure they don't ever face an Employment Tribunal claim.

So, not so much "Would you like fries with that?" More, "We've got vitamins to go with that, and I'm guessing you're not getting them from another firm."

Those are the finite elements that add up to what I call The Money Journey. Those are the rails that make the Cash leg of the stool strong. They trump all strategies and marketing campaigns and the myriad other ways that Partners employ to try to grow their law firms.

Most law firm strategies overlook these basics in their quest for much grander things. Any law firm's 12-month or three-year or five-year strategy should start by looking at all the rails needed by all the legs of the stool, including the elements of The Money Journey.

If you're not doing these things, anything else is a waste of time. Water will just be pouring off the rock.

And you've got to do the above things consistently and for the long term. Pouring buckets of water on a rock changes nothing. A drip onto the rock for many years erodes even granite.

Of course, all of these things are each, and collectively, developing the business of the law firm. They are all forms of "Business Development". Let me take a side road at this juncture so that we can look at what Business Development actually is, and at what is (and at what should be) required of a firm's Partners in Business Development terms.

CHAPTER 13

PARTNERS "DEVELOPING THE BUSINESS"

As the top tier in a law firm, you would naturally expect Partners to be engaged perpetually in developing the business of their firm. Indeed, "Business Development" is an element in every formal Partner-appraisal process and Partner-scorecard system that I have seen. Whereas I have explained previously how "Billing" was removed from the requirements on me, and was replaced by a "Business Development" requirement solely, in most firms the Partners are required to do Business Development *on top of* their billing.

I think "Business Development" has got a bad press amongst Partners and law firms. The picture of what "Business Development" is, is often out of focus. "We want more Business Development from you!" is the demand. Partners respond, but often without guidance, training, or clarity, without effective tools that they can use, and almost always without the many hundreds of hours of Business Development "flying time" that might have taught them what to do and how best to do it.

On paper, Partners doing some Business Development to win new clients sounds right to me. After all, if the Partners aren't going to carry out activities designed to grow the business by winning new clients, who else is? You can't just rely on non-Partners to do it. It's too much, I think, to expect everyone else in the firm to work hard on their own to make the Partners increasingly rich.

Usually, though, "Business Development" is given that narrow meaning by firms, namely "winning new clients". I believe that Partners are indeed the most effective developers of the business when it comes to winning new clients. Not only does their leading by example get others in the firm to do the same, but also because – when they do it – the outside world sees that these are Partners in the firm that's actually being promoted. That has an impact in the same way that we might all be more tempted to buy from a business if we were engaged with – and hearing assurances from – the business owner.

I believe (because I have seen it myself from both ends) that non-Partners doing Business Development "out there" are at a real disadvantage (because they are promoting their employer), and all the more so when they are up against people in the marketplace who can call themselves "Partners" from other firms.

I don't agree, however, that "Business Development" is all about "winning new clients". Rather, I think that it is a multi-headed beast that can take many forms, and many of those forms are effective and valuable. Often, "winning new clients" is a poor result – there are far better results than "winning new clients" that are also a lot easier and cheaper to achieve, and many more Partners can make a valuable Business Development contribution in these other ways than can work a room.

To me, "Business Development" means just that – developing the business so that it better secures necessary sustainable cash-rich and profit-rich growth, year after year. Doesn't that, for example, encompass the Partners and lawyers in the firm all embracing each step of The Money Journey we have looked at? That would certainly develop the business in a range of excellent and sustainable ways. In terms of clients and cases, doesn't "Business Development" mean ensuring the firm makes maximum money on each case and gets maximum cases from every client? Neither of those involves "winning new clients"!

It seems bizarre to me that a Partner can be seen as being great at Business Development when their team's service level is patchy, or the team isn't very profitable and lots of the team's bills are unpaid. It is also curious that firms spend so much time and money on Business Development to "win new clients" when there are thousands of files sitting in the firm awaiting attention and thousands of existing clients that a firm could tap into. There's no point gunning for new clients if you're already too busy, and you're not going to make maximum money from the case, and you're going to treat clients as one-hit wonders.

And more widely than that, doesn't "developing the business" also include all the work that goes into improving IT and into ensuring Compliance, and all the work that goes into the HR function and all the work on the part of the Learning & Development team?

There is no point in winning new clients if you don't have good lawyers to do the work when it needs doing.

This and my other books cover all these aspects, so really, this whole trilogy – in a wider sense – is literally all about Business Development. That is, developing all aspects of the business to arrive at a perfect legal business.

For the purposes of this chapter, though, I will focus on the "winning new clients" side of Business Development.

Within my career in the legal sector, Business Development was my passion. What follows is based on the experience I gained and the lessons I learned in this narrow strand when I was:

1. A non-fee-earning Business Development Partner, as well as being the Director of Business Development and also the Marketing Partner at £50m turnover, full-service law firm Pannone in Manchester, where I had unlimited budgets in terms of time and money.

2. The Managing Partner who led Darbys, another full-service law firm, from being in a turnaround situation during the 2007 Credit Crunch to becoming the UK's fastest-growing law firm.

I put these forward as strong Business Development credentials. I have learned an awful lot of real-world Business Development lessons – more than most, I suspect. Let me share some of those lessons with you.

In looking at effective Business Development that firms (and their Partners) can do, I am going to do this by looking at Business Development in two periods of time.

I am going to look at what typical law firms and their Partners can best do now in terms of Business Development. I am going to call this period, ironically, B.D. That is – we can call this period Before Differentiators.

I do not believe many firms have got any or many firm-wide and concrete differentiators that they can boast of. I looked at these at various stops along The Money Journey earlier. I believe that most of the differentiators that firms boast of are hot air or – because all firms are boasting of the same things – they are not differentiators at all. So, Business Development carried out in this period is bereft of the supercharging that is available by way of concrete differentiators (but as you will see, it can still bear fruit).

After B.D., we will then look at Business Development again in the period A.D. or After Differentiors. Everything changes once a firm (a) has team- or firm-wide, concrete differentiators in place, and (b) they constantly and consistently deliver on them.

Really effective Business Development can now take place, and on a literally industrial scale as so many more people in the team or the firm can effectively contribute to it.

In the Before Differentiators period, I believe that the following are the most basic, most fundamental ways that Partners can do effective Business Development that is aimed at winning new clients, even if the team or the firm doesn't yet have any real, whole-firm, concrete differentiators that it can boast of. The reason that even efforts bereft of such differentiators can still work is that none of your competitors have any real differentiators, either! If they did, you might not fare as well.

These first suggestions are what a firm and its Partners should be doing before anything else. Partners' most basic Business Development comes in the following forms:

- **By recognising opportunities that arise, and responding to them *immediately*.** A firm with a good name will attract callers without a Partner having to do anything specific in terms of marketing or Business Development. Or a call might come in as a result of a Partner doing one or other of the things I mention here. Some calls are dynamite and deserve the investment of some time by a Partner to get the client and the opportunity on board.

  But what if the Partner doesn't ring the caller back? It happens all the time. I talk with receptionists and telephonists at law firms who tell me that lawyers (including Partners) are often terrible at returning calls to new and existing clients. There's no point doing Business Development if we're not even going to call people back. Have you ever seen how hard it is to get a law firm to take a call from a new client?

- **By doing a great job on every file you work on.** Not only will a happy client use you again, and not only will they be open to using all the other teams in your firm, but happy clients will also do an awful lot of your "new client"

Business Development for you. They will join your salesforce. Clients are all engaged in multiple communities – families, affinity groups, sports clubs, golf clubs, business networks, social media groups, pub gatherings, etc. A Partner giving their clients' files the real Push & Tell treatment will soon have their clients flying their flag. It is ironic that some Partners might be unable to deliver a great service all the time because they are out for days on end "doing Business Development". Business Development in the narrow sense of "winning new clients" does not start with a loud, brash personality and the ability to work a busy room, collecting dozens of business cards. Business development begins with the files on your desk.

- **By making small clients into big clients.** Why go looking for new clients when the firm already has thousands of current and lapsed clients you can nurture? Your colleagues in other teams might have dozens of clients you could look at, and you'll have dozens of clients they can look at. And, all the while, a Partner's tendency might be to spend days or evenings at marketing events of some sort in the hope of bumping into one or two potential clients who need their particular work-type. It makes no sense. Making small clients into big clients was how the law firm I led became the UK's fastest-growing firm. I covered this in detail in my first book and have touched on the power of 007 in that book, too. I will give some examples shortly of how I made this work.

- **By raising your profile within the firm.** Yes, *within* the firm, not outside it. If people around your firm know you, know about your expertise, are fond of you, and are proud to be in a firm with you, they will be open to not only responding when an opportunity in your arena crops up, but also to actually talking about you with their clients proactively.

  Keep a low profile, or be abrasive or ungrateful or horrible, or be unreliable, and none of this will happen. Make sure that you deal quickly with every enquiry or opportunity that is referred to you by colleagues, so that they know you'll get them a good name. And *always thank them* and keep them posted on what comes of the referral. A bit of charm goes a long way.

- **By raising your profile "out there".** Some lawyers are naturally high-profile folk that everyone in a town or city knows. They might have a high profile because of their character and energy or because of their involvement in various organisations, charities or communities. Or it might be because they are frequently in the legal or regional (or even national) press. That's not what I'm talking about here. I'll call all that "general" profile-raising. I am referring here to *particular* profile-raising.

  I did it myself from scratch when I launched my law firm Management Consultancy business after I left private practise in 2016. I have now built up nearly 30,000 lawyer connections on LinkedIn, and I regularly do what are (I hope) relevant and interesting posts to my community. Any Partner can do the same – that is, build up a community of their own that is made up of people in their field, whether that be Real Estate professionals or Finance or HR professionals, etc.

There is no excuse for a Partner not having thousands of relevant connections on LinkedIn. They can then do posts themselves or they can share to their communities the posts put out by the firm's marketing team or by their Partners in other teams in the firm. What you are effectively doing here is building your own community where you are the only lawyer and law firm, instead of joining someone else's community where there might be multiple law firms involved.

- **Have a tight network of introducers and referrers.** This opportunity lends itself to some areas of work more than others. Accountants, bankers, surveyors, IFAs, other lawyers in other firms – all of them have clients that might need referring to a Partner. You might not be the only lawyer that each of them might call on, but having a solid rather than a large, casual group of referrers, with whom you keep in regular touch (and whom you never let down when they need you) is a basic Business Development building block. If you – or your colleagues elsewhere in the firm – can refer clients back to them, so much the better.

It's better for a Partner to have a small group of referrers that they try hard to favour with reciprocity, than for a Partner to have, for example, countless lunches with a host of accountants where everyone makes false promises to each other. Less really can be more. This is yet another instance where concrete is better than hot air.

- **By hosting events.** I wouldn't spend much time attending and networking at other people's events. There are usually lots of lawyers from other firms present, and most people at the events are selling. Rather, I'd be hosting my own events (social or educational) that were full of potential buyers and where I was the only lawyer or firm present. Who would I invite? The small existing clients I have mentioned above, the introducers I have mentioned above, my LinkedIn community mentioned above, and clients of the firm whom the gap analysis showed were not yet users of my expertise. This all gives you an audience that you need events for, as opposed to the usual route, which is to design an event and then wonder who you invite to it.

The above, I feel, are the "magnificent seven" essential foundations to a Partner's Business Development efforts where a firm doesn't yet have concrete, all-firm differentiators in place. As you can see, they aren't all about kicking doors in and blowing trumpets. There are many qualitative aspects that all Partners can harness and embrace.

Now, let's look at what happens if you introduce firm-wide, concrete differentiators. Is the A.D. era different? You bet it is! After Differentiators, everything changes. The whole nature of "Business Development" changes, and it did change at my firm.

We no longer had to rely on individual, granular, "micro" efforts. We were now in the "macro" Business Development game – institutionalised, industrial, wholesale, all-firm Business Development.

The differentiators we were able to boast of were :

- **A service pledge**. A promise to clients that we would deliver "A great service – every lawyer, every time". This was a service pledge by absolutely everyone in our firm. And it wasn't just empty words. Using an SMS system, we regularly asked clients how we were doing *during their cases* and whether we were delivering on our service pledge. If any client was unhappy, I (as Managing Partner) would ring that client. We posted the results internally and on the front page of our website. We meant it.

- **We extended all-around care to our clients.** Clients were all enrolled into one or both of our client clubs, of which there was one for individuals and one for businesses. Business owners went into both. No one lawyer or team owned the client – we all owned them. Our marketing and client development programmes engaged with them and raised their awareness of the ways in which we could care for them. No Partner raised the "my client" obstacle to this happening.

- **We didn't just wait for the phone to ring.** We extended proactive care to our clients in the shape of the Platforms I talked about earlier in the book. Our aim was to help clients to avoid trauma and expense down the track.

These differentiators were concrete, not hot air. With them in place, and being delivered on, we no longer need to rely on labour-intensive, individual efforts and initiatives. We actually no longer even needed to rely on winning new clients. Now, everyone in the firm was constantly engaged in Business Development. Everyone trusted everyone to deliver a great service, no one owned clients, and we could all focus on getting clients from Matter 001 to Matter 007 and beyond. And this all works – it works really well.

Everyone was now engaged in Business Development in one way or another. In terms of clients that we already had, our people were delivering a great service, every time. To get those clients to join our sales team and to open up those clients to using us for more things, our staff developed relationships with clients rather than seeing them as transactions. They helped clients to put out fires before they started.

In terms of new clients, all our people knew and were proud of our differentiators, and many more people than the Partners were out there proudly doing "new client" Business Development for us – people from every level and in every part of the firm. They did it because they were proud.

Unless a firm – as a whole – embraces and implements differentiators, they simply cannot come about, and yet the firm requires its Partners to "Do Business

Development" without giving them any real armoury that they can use out there. On one view, this is the firm outsourcing the Business Development challenge to the Partners personally to make up for the firm's shortcomings (in terms of a lack of corporate differentiators) when really it is more within the firm's powers to make the whole Business Development process far more effective and wide-ranging. Again, there needs to be a coming together here, where the firm and its Partners are on the same side and they all work together to take the business on The Money Journey.

Finally, here, I thought it might be valuable to readers if I briefly looked back at my own Business Development days to see what I did and how I did it. To help me make this chapter as valuable as possible to readers, I have listed ten Business Development successes that I enjoyed so you can see what someone who was skilled at Business Development, and who had unlimited budgets in terms of time and money, focused on and was able to achieve for the business.

I am not for one minute saying that I only had successes – believe me, many efforts went completely unrewarded. That's the problem with Business Development. I did have many successes, though. I set some of these out below, not to boast but to underline the broad range of sources that can produce new cases and clients for any firm:

1. My firm did small-scale, infrequent Debt Recovery work for a national entertainment conglomerate. I arranged to meet with the Finance Director to review the files we had on

for them, and to see how we could help them avoid the problems that were cropping up. We ended up getting far more work of that type, plus a huge volume of Commercial and Licensing work. A small client thus became a big client. Most law firms will have dozens, if not hundreds, of clients like this.

The simplest form of "gap analysis" – a table showing your biggest-spending 250 clients – will quickly show you which smaller clients have the potential to become bigger clients, if their fees are divided into the work-types that they have used you for. A client who has paid you £100 (as was the case here) might be written off as small fish, but they could become a big fish with the right nurturing.

2. We received one small Debt Recovery matter for a well-known brewery company. As above, and because I had been given the time and freedom to invest in such initiatives, I arranged to meet with the Finance Director to see what other debts they had on their books and how they could stop more from arising. We built up a huge volume of Debt Recovery work for them, plus a wide range of Commercial and Real Estate work. They then brought a tremendous Corporate job to us, too, but we declined to act on that and advised them to use the much larger firm they'd used in the past. Again, a small client became a big client.

3. A new junior solicitor at our firm came with an interesting contact. It was unclear at that time what the opportunity was. To support the new solicitor, I went with her to meet and talk things through with the contact. I involved relevant people in my firm, then I dropped out. The resulting relationship with that client was worth £millions to the firm. This is a good example of where Partners supporting junior lawyers is great for everyone. It was great for the firm, and guess how the junior lawyer felt.

4. The great Rodger Pannone had long talked about his "hub and spoke" idea, where a large law firm supported smaller law firms to help them deliver a wide range of legal services to their clients. He and I explored this and imagined how this concept could be strengthened and grown. In due course, we launched the Connect2Law network for law firms. Supported in this roll-out by the Managing Partner and by my Equity Partners, I lived out of the boot of my car (not literally) as I travelled the country visiting law firms. Literally thousands of law firms signed up. The scheme became national and franchised, bringing £millions of fees per year into the firm.

5. Whereas my fee-earning Partners had billing targets, I set myself "client" targets. I wanted to land a particular household-name company that was from my home town as a client for my firm.

I identified their insurance broker and asked for an introduction to the client. The broker went the extra mile, and I spent some incredible time over a weekend with the Managing Director of the target company. I was desperate to sell to him, but I didn't, until late on the Sunday night when he said to me, "So, Simon – you're a lawyer. What do you do?" My reply was, "I take your call late on a Sunday night, but you've probably already got someone who does that, don't you?" He didn't have anyone like that, and the following morning, what can only be described as a torrent of Commercial and Private Work started pouring in, as it was diverted from a range of law firms who were not giving that client the service they deserved at the time.

6. Our Employment team ran a really impressive and popular programme of workshops and seminars for our Corporate clients and their target clients. I used to attend them all to try to convert targets and to widen our relationship with existing Employment clients. One such target was an e-commerce company that was growing, and looking for Venture Capital funding. They instructed us on that fundraising, and thus began a very lucrative relationship for my firm. And for me, personally, as I met my wife there!

7. On a Thursday night, I attended an event hosted by a firm of accountants. The following morning, Friday, a Partner at the accountancy firm very kindly rang me to say that he had a

client with him at that moment who needed an injunction to stop a commercial property disposal that was due to take place on the Monday. I got a team together in our office, and the accountant brought the client around straight away. Our lawyers worked all weekend, got the injunction, and then embarked on a long and lucrative multi-team journey with that client.

8. One client that I had looked after asked if I might give some time to one of his business contacts, the owner of an automotive business. The client had done the selling to that owner for us. Of course I would! The owner came to my office armed with numerous files, each relating to a legal matter they were involved in. They were unhappy with their existing lawyers, and we became their go-to lawyers for everything.

9. At another firm, we had a Notary Public. The list of international companies for which they carried out notarial work was unbelievable. I set up a system with the Notary whereby, to the Notary's enormous credit, I was introduced by them to the company each time – and it was usually someone high-up in each company. I would arrange to go and meet them to listen to their needs in law firm terms, and I made no bones about our desire and our ability to replace their existing lawyers. The first success from this teamwork came when one of the companies I had visited rang me to say they needed a

commercial lawyer, so I made an introduction to one of my colleagues who got to work for the new client.

10. Working with another Partner in the firm, we ran a workshop in our city centre offices at lunchtime for businesses, called "How to Avoid Litigation… or, If You Can't Avoid it, How To Win It". Take-up was really good and we got various clients from it. The first was a call from a company director who had been at the very first of these workshops. He rang with a city centre commercial property job.

One note of caution when talking about Business Development – there is actually a danger that even where Business Development appears to be successful, it ultimately does the firm no good at all. If the firm is going to bill £10m anyway, and the Partners' Business Development efforts don't help it to bill more than that, what is the point? All too often, Business Development merely brings in more cases that an already busy team can't fully deal with. The secret to making Business Development actually pay is to make sure the firm has the capacity to receive and to fully deal with new cases so that – in this example – the firm bills £12m instead of the expected £10m. It's not just about making maximum money on cases – it's about making maximum money soon.

In summary, as you can see, a firm that presses Partners to "Do Business Development" can produce results. And in ways wider than you might have thought possible, if all Partners manage to get the "magnificent seven" basics in place. That individual-level Business Development cannot be a game-changer, though. It tops things up and keeps the firm busy. The game-changer comes from each and every Partner – and crucially the firm itself and as a whole – embracing each step of The Money Journey, including the first step, the design and launch of some all-firm differentiators. That will bring you firmly into the After Differentiators era.

And you'd make maximum money out of each case, soon, and you'd get maximum cases out of each client, and you'd have new clients galore trying to get over your high bar.

So, narrow Business Development (i.e., winning new clients) is not a game-changer. If some or even many of the Partners in a firm did the wider Business Development things, such as embracing all aspects of The Money Journey, there would undoubtedly be solid business progress. But if *every* Partner really did them, and did them all – all the time – there would also be a monumental side-effect.

There would be a destiny-changing impact on the business as a result of the injection of the magic ingredient. The stars would be within reach.

CHAPTER 14

THE MAGIC INGREDIENT

In this book, I know I talk about such lofty things as the Moon and the stars, but I genuinely wouldn't write a book where a series of unattainable steps led to an unattainable dream. I simply wouldn't enjoy writing about something where the chances of any real success were slim. It's just not what I do.

Instead of wasting readers' time in that way, I believe I have mapped out a series of simple, sensible, credible steps, where success is possible if a series of rails are laid down by the Partners and adhered to by the firm.

However, with the addition of what I have been calling "the magic ingredient", destiny-changing success is at your fingertips. Those rails become electrified!

The basic rails are good, but the magic ingredient is truly a great thing, for it magnifies, amplifies, and exponentially increases the good that can come from steps being taken that would otherwise have a more local and limited impact.

I hope you will accept the validity and wisdom of many or most (or even all) of the "things" or rails I have discussed so far. If you put them all in place, however, (and all in place at the same time and joined up), that actually only gets you to the start line of the journey to a new destiny, and maybe a bit beyond that start line. In achieving all of this, you will already stand out from most law firms, your clients will benefit, and you will make more money. Why not go further, though? So far, you'd be going around your usual orbit a bit faster and a bit higher. Why don't we instead go for the Moon? See those stars? They're up for grabs.

Yes, it's time to break free of the bonds that make up 'the old way'. Come on, let's go 'full thrust'! It's time to unhook all the cables and chains and weights that have kept us going around and around the same planet for decades.

Let's go into this with our eyes open, though. Let's build failure – and a way of dealing with it – into our plans. We need to bear in mind a particular feature of law firms, Partners, and lawyers. That is, *our propensity to deviate quite quickly from an agreed plan or route.*

Remember the lawyers I talked about with their full heads, with little or no room for new things? That applies here, too. Sticking to the handful of rails that I identify in this book, week after week, month after month, and year after year, can get boring for lawyers. I often see an initial focus on the new rails drift off as old ways return or as heads turn towards new, apparently more exciting things. The gravity that has kept you in the old orbit for years will slowly but surely pull you back down to Earth if the rocket's engines only burn for a short time. We need to keep them firing.

The challenges, therefore, when we are trying to change a law firm's direction and speed of travel (that is, its destiny) are:

1. Knowing what to do – what should our rails be?

2. Genuinely challenging yourself and, where relevant, accepting that you need to do some or many things differently.

3. Implementing the necessary changes – that is, making decisions and taking action rather than talking things to death, and generating concrete rails rather than hot air. In short, agreeing what rails the firm is going to get onto.

4. Implementing the rails all at the same time and in a joined-up way.

5. Moving forward constantly and consistently along all the rails.

6. Not being bored by things that become less-than-exciting or being distracted by new shiny things that you see or hear about, or that you see or hear or fear other firms are doing.

Moving towards a new destiny in this way can be a monotonous journey, but if you do it all, as a team, and without relenting, it is a journey that is certain to succeed. The amazing thing is that all of the above challenges are overcome by the one, magic ingredient that I have referred to throughout this book.

It's called *Leadership*.

In law firms, you can get some people to do some things for some of the time. You achieve that by having bosses that tell people what to do.

You're always going to get some success for a period of time when a boss gives out an order.

But, I'm sorry, as an industry, we've been relying on that flawed system for too long. We might once have got away with the limited results it produced. Not any longer. Direct Costs and Overheads are now so high (and they can change horribly overnight) that we now need *all the people doing all the right things all the time.*

You can try to achieve that by dishing out louder and more regular demands of your people, and by attaching stiff penalties or sanctions for non-compliance. That still won't be enough, though. In that environment, people will typically do the minimum to avoid breaking the rules, and they'll do the minimum to look like they are compliant. People will draw comfort from the fact that they are not the worst in the firm, rather than aspiring to pride in being the best.

As well as not being effective in getting the desired results, that kind of regime – where Management's barking gets louder and more regular – delivers a far from uplifting culture and enjoyable work experience. There is no heart for everyone to buy into.

No, we need something radically different to a system based on bosses – bosses who, of course, are appointed by other bosses to be bosses. We've tried the "boss" system. It has failed. In essence, rather than telling people what to do, so that they do the minimum, let's get them *wanting* to do the necessary things and to want to do them *to the maximum.*

A law firm needs to replace the "boss" system with something far more effective. That "something" can indeed come from the people who are currently bosses, but it is not limited to them. It can come from anywhere, at any level.

I am talking about leadership. I'm not a great reader around "Leadership" or around "business" in general. I think I have only ever read one book on these things. I don't listen to podcasts or watch Ted Talks on them, either. I deliberately don't go to events where leadership gurus or other legal sector Management Consultants are talking. That's their livelihood and I don't want to benefit from their hard work and from the years they have invested.

In light of this, you will either think that my views are uninformed or disconnected from mainstream thought leaders, or you might think that my views – which are based on my vast direct experiences – are an independent, free-standing set of views that you can add to the mix. I hope you do.

Let's turn to Partners. Is a Partner in a law firm a "leader"? The Partners might immediately think of and see themselves as the leadership group in that firm, but no, they are absolutely not automatically the leadership group. Rather, they are the "bosses" group.

No one can be designated or appointed a leader. Leadership can come from anyone at any level in the firm – and they aren't and don't need to be appointed as leaders. Over the decades, I have seen many Partners who could never be called a leader. And I have seen many junior people who have demonstrated real leadership qualities and impact, even though they had no formal power or authority at all.

A good law firm ought to look at where its actual leadership is coming from – and the people who are delivering it ought to be brought into the sunlight and watered (and rewarded). Just because you are a boss, it doesn't mean you are a leader. Just because you aren't a boss, it doesn't mean you can't be a leader.

Although the Partners in a law firm aren't the only ones who can behave like, and therefore be, leaders, it should be an absolute requirement by the firm that each and every Partner embraces and exhibits leadership traits.

Leadership should come from each and every one of the Partners individually and from the partnership group as a whole. If you don't get the former, it's simply not possible to have the latter. Even one single Partner, by way of their behaviours, can sink the entire Leadership boat, as it is only when every single Partner is acting like a leader that we can have the real "blast off" that is attainable here.

So, what do I mean by "Leadership" within a law firm environment? I mean something quite specific and concrete. I mean that:

1. A Partner needs to exhibit what I am calling Leadership Behaviours that get the people around them to look at them in a positive way.

2. If those Leadership Behaviours are exhibited consistently, the people around the Partner will begin to respect and trust the Partner.

3. The people around that Partner will become open to being influenced by them.

4. If the Partner is focused and trained and incentivised to consistently act in specific ways that are beneficial to the business and everyone in it, and they are committed to spreading their good works by engaging with the people around them to promote these ways, then – because they are trusted influencers – people around them will

do these good things, too. Partners can achieve solid progress here by exhibiting Leadership Behaviours, by leading by example, and by taking what I am calling *Leadership Actions*.

That is a very simple, honest, and very human explanation of my view as to how you can lead people in a new and good direction in a law firm. May I emphasise two points:

- If a Partner does not exhibit Leadership Behaviours, it is "game over" for that Partner. They will remain a boss.

- If one Partner acts as, and therefore remains, a boss, the entire Partner group can lose the opportunity to be an effective *leadership* group.

Whilst I believe this is how leadership arises, and I have lots of experience of seeing it happen, I can't guarantee that people will follow the leader in every case. I *can* guarantee, though, how to make sure no one will ever follow the "leader".

Watch what happens if the boss does the opposite of the things I have set out:

- If the boss is simply horrible, it all breaks down at 1. (above)

- If the boss is sometimes nice, but horrible at other times, it breaks down at 2. (above)

- If the boss consistently behaves like a leader but then does nothing with that influence, or they lead people in the wrong direction, it breaks down at 4.

Having Leadership Behaviours is a good start (in fact, it is the only start) but is not enough. The Partner who becomes a leader by consistently exhibiting Leadership Behaviours then has to add in some Leadership Actions before they can become a positive *and active* leader, and an influencer over the people around them. That's when everyone does – and wants to do – all the things that the business needs. And to do them to the maximum, not the minimum.

In short, we need each Partner to satisfy the needs of each of the four "leadership" steps listed just above. We will take the Leadership Behaviours first, and turn to Leadership Actions later.

The first step in building and developing a leader in a law firm (and, specifically here, in ensuring that a Partner is not just a boss but is also a leader) is to get the Partner to consistently exhibit the good "people" behaviours that get the people around them to look at them positively. We are aiming for the people around them to respect and trust them. If there is no trust and no respect, there is no chance whatsoever of people agreeing to be led anywhere by the Partner. Thus, we need to look specifically at how – in a law firm environment – trust and respect for Partners arises.

You will see straight away that we have left the realms of judging the value of a Partner to a firm in terms of their profile, or their abilities as a technical lawyer, or their billing performance, or in terms of their Business Development skills. Each of those skills adds something to a law firm, yes, but absent the qualities that we are about to look at, a Partner's contribution to a business is limited and may even cross the line into being negative rather than positive, when you look at what their individual behaviours can ultimately *deprive* a law firm of. I have seen and heard of countless examples of high-performing Partners, who were actually nightmares and who – rather than pushing the overall business forward – were actually and acutely holding it back. They were not only keeping it chained to the gravity of the old planet, but they were also jeopardising its ability to carry on safely orbiting even that old planet.

It is tempting, when looking at the Partner qualities and behaviours that give rise to trust and respect (that in turn give birth to leadership situations), to talk about "good leaders" and "bad leaders". That is a nonsense. You don't have "bad leaders". They are simply not leaders. There are only ever good leaders. If you are a "bad" leader, then you aren't a leader, you're a boss.

It is hard to believe some of the stories that I hear from junior lawyers around the world, even now. Ranging from things I have seen and heard myself, to the many incredible stories I heard, including during my interviews for this book (and you will see some of these when I turn to those interviews), you cannot imagine these things still go on.

Those behaviours are so far removed from the magic that can be worked by Partners acting in the right way. You may have heard of the social experiment that was carried out where teachers at a school were told that some particular students were absolute shining stars and were likely to be the ones to make it big out of that student group. Guess what – they did. But also guess what – there was nothing special about the named students at all. It was simply that the teachers being told certain students were special led them to treat the pupils differently, and that made those pupils believe in themselves. That's what Partners can do to the people around them.

Some Partner behaviours (and I don't just mean extreme ones) not only mean that leadership by that Partner won't ever arise – they also mean that there can never be any leadership in the firm as a whole. That's because the people as a unit don't trust and respect the partnership as a group. *The Partner group is judged by the behaviours of its worst member.* So the firm, as ever, has a role to play here. You can have a majority of Partners adopting Leadership Behaviours religiously, but it's not those "good" Partners that will show the internal and external worlds what the firm is truly like. That power falls to two other parties:

- First, to those Partners who exhibit bad behaviours.

- Second, to the firm's Senior Management, if it tolerates those bad behaviours.

It is these things that tell the internal and external world what a firm and a partnership is like. It's not the good behaviours you have secured on the part of most Partners that define whether cross-partnership leadership (and a good culture) exists in the firm. It's whether the firm tolerates rogue, bad behaviours.

These bad behaviours can be one-off, or they can be a pattern. If the firm tolerates them, though, there is no culture of leadership, is there? Is it one rule for everyone, or can you behave like you want if you're an Equity Partner, say, or a big biller?

The presence of extreme behaviours can kill leadership, but so too can the mere and less dramatic *absence* of some good behaviours. Let's look at the behaviours that need to be exhibited by a Partner if they are to cross the bridge and become a leader instead of just being a boss.

CHAPTER 15

BUILDING TRUST AND RESPECT – LEADERSHIP BEHAVIOURS

Tailored specifically to the law firm environment, I now turn to the Leadership Behaviours that I believe generate the respect for, and the trust of, a Partner.

They are the foundations from which leadership can rise.

These Leadership Behaviours are light years away from the complete lack of mettle that you saw in Chapter 1, and from many of the Partner behaviours described in the interviews below.

My thoughts here come from the countless interactions and experiences I had with Partners when I was a junior lawyer. My thoughts also come from the thousands of experiences my friends and colleagues in the profession have shared with me over the years (because, of course, junior people in law firms talk – *a lot*), and from thousands of conversations I have had with lawyers at all levels in the decade or so of my law firm Management Consultancy work.

LEADERSHIP BEHAVIOURS

Be authentic	There is no "Leader" template. Be yourself.
Be polite	Everyone is entitled to dignity at work, whatever they've done
Be empathetic	You get a lot further with honey than you do with vinegar
Be calm	Shouting and anger mean "game over" in leadership terms
Be fair	Treat everyone the same. Don't have "favourites"
Build relationships	With everyone. Give each person time. And you can't do that just by email.
Be adaptable	We're all different. Learn what makes each person tick. One size…, etc
Be ambitious	People won't follow someone who doesn't want to take things somewhere
Communicate	Don't be a black hole. Share the ups and downs. Talk to everyone
Poor performers	No one will step up for you if you tolerate poor performers – have a high bar

Be decisive	People respect courage in decision-making
Don't be a "yes" person	You can (and must) say "No", but with empathy
Listen	Don't just talk. Ask for views. Allow and embrace disagreements
Own your decisions	No one expects them all to be right, but don't run away from the wrong ones
Action!	Don't just be a talking shop
Deliver!	Do what you say you are going to do
Bring islands together	Working as a team is more effective and more fun
Team environment	Ask for views, and listen. That creates a team culture from the top
Operate as a team	Allocate tasks and roles – people love being given responsibility
Trust and empower people	Let them make decisions as you can't make them all. That's how people learn
Accountability	Everyone needs to be accountable, or people will see it as a joke

Mistakes are great	Allow mistakes, celebrate them, and help your people learn from them
Move on!	Don't dwell on negatives. Learn, and all move on
Be organised	Would you put your career into the hands of someone who is chaotic?
Be accessible	Your door may be open – but are people scared to walk through?
Be reasonable	Someone's evenings or weekends are important to them
Give credit. Say thank you	And publicly. Take the blame, share the fame
A plan for each person	Does each person believe you have your eye on their progression?
Deliver on that plan	Make sure that they are getting the time and training they need to develop
Celebrate "people" success	Let everyone see that you are committed to the growth of your people
Be sustained and consistent	Flashes in the pan won't fool anyone

Ask for feedback – on you	Asking the team for feedback on you (and acting on it) reinforces leadership

Whether a Partner has one junior lawyer around them, or lots, or whether or not the Partner is actually a Team Leader or Head of Department, the need to exhibit these Leadership Behaviours is the same. The aim at this stage is always the same.

That is, to get everyone willing and wanting to be led, to get everyone trusting and identifying their local leader, and to get everyone working together as a team, all rowing in the same and right direction.

Would these basic human behaviours (that is, Leadership Behaviours) push your buttons? Would these things make you think that a Partner was decent, honest, and fair? Would these things help you to respect them? Would these things help you to trust them? I believe they would.

Alas, I only have to spend a few seconds looking back at my own experiences in law firms and at the myriad "Partner" stories that have been shared with me over the years, to see that much on the above list is wishful thinking. Much of the time, Partner behaviours simply get nowhere near creating the fertile, respect-rich and trust-rich ground needed for the green shoots of leadership to sprout. Instead, all too often, Partners are pressing all the wrong buttons:

THE WRONG BUTTONS

Focusing on me, me, me	Don't always talk about "I" – talk about "we"
Celebrating yourself	Celebrate others' achievements, not your own
Being rude or charmless	Abrasive interactions with a boss crush people
Shouting at staff	Really?
Do as I say!	Don't only be concerned with your own views – ask others
Dismissing disagreements	People will simply switch off
Lacking ambition	People won't follow you if you're not going anywhere
Being inaccessible	Be an open door, and more than in just name
Not delegating tasks	Don't trust anyone to do anything? They'll see it as a dead end
Talking rather than listening	If you just talk at people, they'll sit in silence – disconnected
Playing the blame game	Blaming people kills trust. It's a downright horrible trait
Being indecisive	Who's going to follow someone who never decides anything?

Being afraid to say "No"	A "Yes" to everything fools no one. Leaders know how to say "No", too
Being inconsistent	Which boss are they going to get today?
Having favourites	Pop goes the leadership balloon
Not giving honest feedback	Saying nice things that you don't mean helps no one
Looking like a mess	As above – would you put your career in the hands of a chaotic boss?
Being a black hole	Do things go into your office/inbox and never come out?
Dwelling on mistakes	Learn from them and move on – show them their boss supports them
Taking credit	Horrible. Unforgiveable
Being in bad moods	Horrible. Pop
Inappropriate comments	Pop
The silent treatment	There's no difference between this and shouting at people. Pop
Micro-managing	Pop. Let them get on with the tasks and make mistakes.
Gossiping	Pop

Tolerating poor performance	Pop
Unreliable	If you never do what you say you'll do – pop

Pop, pop, pop. You get the picture. Can you imagine how these behaviours make a lawyer or lawyers feel?

That's the acid test here. They say lawyers don't leave firms; they leave their boss. To a large degree, I agree with that. They leave when there have been too many pops.

Leadership Behaviours turn a Partner from a boss into a leader. It's not my wording, but I very much like the saying that sums this up, "When I talk with my boss, it feels like they're important. When I talk with our leader, it feels like I'm important."

During the very many discussions I have had over the years with lawyers around the world, including for this book, I can see that many of these wrong behaviours are still commonplace in the legal profession – and in some extreme forms. And at firms that boast of "great cultures". You can see some examples in the interviews that I come to later.

I'm sorry, but if even one Partner in a firm behaves in any of these ways, and is allowed by Senior Management to do so, then the firm has no "great culture", and it will miss the "leadership" boat. A great culture is 100% or 0%. You can't have a great culture for some of the time in some parts of the firm.

Bad Partner behaviours (even by one Partner) ruin a great culture, but they also ruin any chance of wider leadership truly arising in the firm. Bad Partner behaviours (and behaviours don't need to be extreme to be bad) are extremely costly to a legal business. Lawyers (and as one, I know) need to be treated in a certain way. But absolutely everyone in a firm deserves to be treated well. Ignore that at your peril.

Let's look at one moment in the life of a lawyer when they know – instantly – whether they ought to stay with their boss.

The moment I am talking about is the lawyer's formal appraisal. Some firms don't hold these at all. That may be because the firm prefers to have ongoing, informal discussions with its people instead. Or it may be because chaos reigns and the firm has no "people" strategy in place.

I firmly believe in ongoing discussions, but I believe there is real value in a formal appraisal structure, too. My preference is for there to be one appraisal straight after each financial year-end (so that a lawyer's direct and indirect contribution to the business, and their development during the previous financial year, can be discussed, and so that plans can be made for the year ahead) and for there to be a half-year appraisal six months into the new financial year, to ensure both parties are giving what the other needs.

These appraisals are Heaven-sent opportunities for Partners to demonstrate a range of the Leadership Behaviours I have identified above. What a great opportunity to focus on the employee and their development, to show them that the Partner has a plan for them and an interest in them. What a great moment for a leader to reinforce their leadership credentials, to show that they are deserving of the employee's trust, respect, and confidence.

Sadly, though, formal appraisals have got a bad name in many quarters. Thinking back to some appraisals that I had to endure during my career, I know why. When they take place, they can be soulless, directionless, cold, form-filling exercises.

All the appraisee might see is the top of the appraiser's head as they mechanically tick boxes on a lengthy pro forma document.

The appraiser often shows their shallow interest in the employee's career by having their mobile phone out on the table, the phone's presence indicating that – at any moment – someone far more important than the employee might draw the Partner away.

Even if they take place, there is often little that comes from them. That is the firm as a whole ensuring that leadership – at a local or firm-wide level – cannot develop or survive.

And that's all if the appraisals actually take place. Often, the Partner tasked with carrying out appraisals doesn't get around to doing them. "Too busy." Or they are done at the last minute and in a rush because the Lexcel inspector is visiting the firm. What does all that tell the employees about their boss's care for them and their development? There can literally be no leadership when the boss can't set aside time to talk about the one thing that every employee wants (totally reasonably) to talk about – themselves and their future.

And what does it say about the firm as a whole when such an abject failure by a Partner or Partners is allowed to carry on? I regularly come across HR teams who despair because all their good work is going up in smoke because Partners don't do the appraisals allocated to them.

I, therefore, say this to Partners who are too busy to do their appraisals – that shocking failure to focus on your people and their development is having a terrible impact on your standing and on the entire business. At best, leadership by you individually is literally impossible, and leadership by the Partner group as a whole is weakened. Your saddened, demotivated people will be talking about you in disparaging terms and they are more likely to leave you and leave the firm. You may think it's a small thing. Take it from me – it's a huge thing for you, your team, and your firm.

By consistently pressing the right buttons, and by consistently exhibiting Leadership Behaviours, a Partner can earn trust and respect. The "boss" becomes a "leader".

A word of warning, though… leadership is hard to create but very easy to lose. A leader is always in danger of losing the trust and respect they have worked hard to create.

One reversal of any Leadership Behaviour can cause real damage to the leader. One lapse might show the people that the leader was just a boss in disguise. Contrition and reform can rebuild the trust and respect (and perhaps even strengthen it), whether the Partner does this of their own volition or in concert with (and at the direction of) Senior Management. If there is a transgression, and neither the Partner nor the firm does anything to remedy the situation and rebuild trust, the balloon may have popped. Never let your guard down, and constantly examine how you are doing as a leader – including by asking the team for feedback on you.

With consistent Leadership Behaviours being exhibited, we can now move on to the next stage, namely Leadership Actions. Leadership Behaviours on their own make the firm a good place to work. The law firm, though, is a business, and if we want to achieve great things and get to the Moon and the stars, we need Leadership Actions.

Absent Leadership Actions, we would have created a Partner who has the respect and trust of others around them, who has brought a small or large group together where the group can work as a team and is willing to be led in a certain direction (and almost certainly wants to be led in a certain direction), but the leader isn't necessarily leading those people anywhere.

And a leader cannot lead in just any direction – it has to be the right direction. There's no point being a leader, even a great leader, if you don't lead people anywhere, or if you lead them in the wrong direction!

Speaking personally, I genuinely believe I had some good leadership qualities and skills when I was the Managing Partner. I must have done, or we wouldn't have got where we got.

However, where I led people to was downright wrong in a number of respects. I own that mistake. I'm genuinely sorry to all my people for the missed opportunity. I didn't know then what I know now about sustainably growing a law firm in the right profit-rich and cash-rich ways. Hence my evangelism now around helping law firms to do the things that I did right but also to avoid doing the things that I did wrong.

Let's now look at the Leadership Actions that are required once a leadership situation has arisen.

CHAPTER 16

LEADERSHIP ACTIONS – THE BRAINSTORM

Having transitioned from a boss to a leader, the leader can't rest on their laurels and must instead now actively use the happy "leadership" state of affairs that has arisen for the benefit of the business and everyone in it.

They must use their new-found leadership status to get the people around them to do all the right things, in the right way, all the time. Leadership Actions are now needed.

Let's now move on and look at how the leader needs to harness and use their leadership status for the benefit of the business.

"Leadership" is not an end in itself – it is the means to a much greater end.

Leadership Actions involve the leader now doing certain business things themselves in the right way and all the time, and it involves the leader engaging with their people on an ongoing basis to inspire and lead them to do these things all the time, too. The real business value in leadership is *leverage*. One Partner changing and doing things better can help the business a bit. One leader who gets others to do things right all the time is the game-changer.

The required Leadership Actions are as follows:

- There needs to be a clear vision and plan

- The vision and plan need to be ambitious

- The leader must believe in the vision and plan

- The leader must demand high performance from their people

- The leader must lead by example

- The leader needs to instil Leadership Behaviours across the team

- The leader must use a range of tools to launch the new direction, to actually make things happen, *and to keep them happening*

This is the case whether there is a small issue to be dealt with in a team, or a wider, major planning and business improvement exercise is needed.

Let's look at each part of this.

The plan? Let's imagine that we want to boost the business performance of the team and the firm in all the ways we have looked at in this book.

The actual plan depends on the position of the leader in question, as there can be multiple plans at different levels, all based on the same business pillars:

- If you are mainly a fee-earning Partner, and you have a junior lawyer or lawyers allocated to assist you, or you don't have a dedicated "lieutenant" but you can call upon a range of junior lawyers in your team, the first part of the plan must be work-type- and client-focused

- If you are the head of a team, then the plan becomes more complex as its aim is to secure change on the part of a group of people with whom you are not personally working on client files day-to-day

In each of these situations, though, the plans have to align. It does not work if Partner A in a team leads their people in one direction, but Partner B tries to lead the wider team in another. There needs to be a dovetailing of the various levels of the plan so that the many strands come together to form a strong cable.

The dovetailing that is needed comes from the fact that – in all these cases – the key themes that I have talked about are at the root of each plan. There is no conflict between plans at the various levels within the firm, and all the plans get over the "ambition" bar, as the ambition is (of course) to shoot for the Moon and the stars on a team level and on a firm level.

Let's start with the first and simplest of these plans – the fee-earning Partner who has one or more junior lawyers working with them on client matters.

With the Leadership Behaviours we listed above being exhibited consistently by the Partner, trust and respect will be engendered in a junior lawyer.

The junior lawyer is thus open to being influenced and led by the Partner. The Partner who exhibits Leadership Behaviours and also embraces the disciplines I set out in The Money Journey, and who leads by example on all those fronts, then embarks on that Money Journey, taking the junior lawyers with them. Leadership here is not in a vacuum – we need the Partner to adhere to the rails that are within The Money Journey that will strengthen the Cash leg of the stool:

- Having pride in pricing and ensuring that the cases taken on benefit two sides, not one

- Retainers are defined, and the engagement with clients is an exacting one

- Delivering a service to clients where you always push the case and always tell the client

- Raising any work that is needed that is outside the initial scope with clients immediately

- Capturing every minute that is spent on client files

- Billing every minute that is recorded, or using that data to raise your fixed prices

- Getting the cash in quickly

- Seeing the client as a client for the whole firm, not just as a case for you

- Wanting to extend proactive care from across the firm to the clients you are working for

Just imagine if every Partner in a firm did these things all the time.

But more than that – just imagine if, in doing so within the wrapper of Leadership Behaviours and in leading by example, the Partners in the firm were able to bring *all the lawyers they worked with* into these ways, too. The sound of balloons popping and of baths draining would soon be replaced by the sound of rocket engines firing up.

Let's now move up a level and look at what a leader can do where they are already in some form of management position, such as a Team Leader. For "management position", you can often read "boss", where the boss tells people what to do. People don't always do what they are told, of course.

Bosses and managers are not automatically leaders. They might even be called a leader – e.g., Team Leader. That title counts for nothing.

History is littered with Team Leaders who never led anyone anywhere. Instead of leading a team forwards and upwards, they can destroy teams and take them backwards and downwards.

The Team Leader needs to establish leadership by behaving in all the leadership ways we have looked at. They then need to use that leadership across a wider group, for the benefit of the team and the whole business.

A first Leadership Action for them is to ensure that there is a *clear plan for the team*. And it must be a plan that is *ambitious*.

The leader cannot dictate what the plan is, though. Remember the "Bad" behaviour above, namely "Do as I say", and the "Good" behaviour, namely "Ask and listen"? The team has to design the plan. For "plan", read rails.

To a great degree, what happens in law firms is more the bad behaviour – for example, emails from the Team Leader or from Senior Management saying, "Get your billing up!" or "Record more time!" or "Get your bills paid!"

What is needed in a law firm is the Partner who leads any group of any size to recognise that a moment is upon them – a moment when "the old" can be discarded. Where there is an opportunity for the team to raise their sights and aim even higher. It is a moment to leave the status quo behind and to change up a gear that will be to the benefit of everyone in the team. No more going around in the same orbit. It's Moon time.

A right-thinking team will be joyous at the thought of the person leading them wanting to lead them somewhere special, and will be joyous at being asked to help design the plan and the team's rails.

The leader, having recognised that there is an opportunity for blast-off, needs to launch the project with their team to examine the opportunity and to craft the actions, skills, priorities, and behaviours (that is, the rails) needed to ignite the fuel.

What is needed now is a good, old-fashioned team *brainstorm*. Calling and facilitating and catalysing that brainstorm are key Leadership Actions.

A team brainstorm is very different to a team meeting where a boss talks at everyone. And it's not too wide-ranging a discussion. As the aims are to build a sustainable and growing team business that is good for the team's members, the team's clients, and for the firm and the business as a whole, the areas to brainstorm in order to arrive at the team's rails are simply:

1. How do we – as a team – strengthen all four legs of the stool?

2. How do we – as a team – deliver for the long
   term on all the parts that make up The Money
   Journey?

Nothing else matters.

It is likely that a leader-led team discussion around
these questions will identify similar themes and
opportunities to those we have looked at so far:

Leg of the stool	Rails needed?
Clients	How do we deliver great legal expertise and push all cases, all the time?
	How do we ensure that we always tell the clients where their case is up to?
	Do we need more or different resources or lawyers?
	What do we want from our clients in return? Let's raise the bar
	Let's recognise that colleagues in other teams can care for these clients, too
Compliance	What are the rules that apply to us?
	How can we comply with them fully, smoothly, and efficiently?

Leg of the stool	Rails needed?
Colleagues	Let's ensure we have the full range of Leadership Behaviours across the team We can protect well-being by doing less, better, for more What training and development does each colleague want and need?
Cash	Let's individually and collectively – as a team – embrace every aspect of The Money Journey!

In dismantling how the team operates for the benefit of clients, and in dismantling the cogs that move the team machine from the delivery of legal expertise to the generation of maximum profit and cash for the business, the team might come up with some or all of the priorities and rails that I mention.

They might, though – and hopefully they will – come up with different and wider ideas tailored to them and their team. That's all the better! I don't profess to having all the answers, and nor can the team's leader. In true Leadership Behaviour style, the meeting is all about examining, involving, discussing, and listening.

The leader doesn't have to try to please everyone in the brainstorm by including every rail suggested by the team during the discussion in the final plan. "Trying to please everyone" is something we could add to the

"Bad behaviours" list above. As Steve Jobs of Apple fame said, "If you want to make everyone happy, don't be a leader, sell ice cream."

Instead, the leader has to ask, listen, sort, and prioritise. The leader needs to be able to say "no" or "not now". Empathy and gratitude when they do is also a good idea.

The first Leadership Action we need to see, therefore, is the launching of the brainstorm and the leading of the discussion.

The second is the arrival with the team at a set of measures agreed by the team as their new priorities. These priorities are our *rails*.

The team designed them, and the team – the whole team – owns them and needs to embrace, push, and defend them. The team then needs to move along those rails. This is where the next Leadership Actions come in.

Acting as a leader and having a team identify good rails, stick to them, and move nicely along them is the best and biggest contribution that a law firm can see from its Partners. It beats personal billing, hands down.

If a Partner doesn't adopt Leadership Behaviours, or does adopt them but then – as a leader – doesn't follow them up with Leadership Actions to get their people to identify and then move along agreed rails, then everything falls flat. In either case (in light of the fact that a firm has to grow every year to even stand still) that Partner is literally forcing Senior Management to seek our far more costly, risky, and generally doomed ways to achieve the growth that is needed.

Pausing there, now that we've looked at the required Leadership Behaviours and Leadership Actions, how do you think Partners do, generally? Do they exhibit Leadership Behaviours? Sadly, "No" is often the answer – and you don't need to just take it from me.

CHAPTER 17

WHAT THE PEOPLE SAY

Everything you have seen and read so far has been made up of my views based on my experiences. However, I wanted to go further in this book and listen very carefully to people engaged in law firms at various levels to see what they felt made The Perfect Partner, and to hear what their experiences of Partners actually were.

I started by talking to a range of people who occupy the seat that I once sat in – the hot seat, as I call it. They had a range of titles – Managing Partner, Chief Executive Officer, or Managing Director. Here, I simply label them all "Managing Partner". Here are some of the thoughts of some of the Managing Partners I spoke with.

Managing Partner

"All Partners should be on the same page, should be able to talk maturely as a group, and need to collaborate as a group. They should lead by example.

It's unfair if they want the staff to act and behave in a certain way. There aren't two sets of rules. There should be no exceptions to complying with policies.

We often see two sets of rules – Partners coming and going as they want, thinking that "rules don't apply to me". They treat the whole thing as a lifestyle that's built around them.

We have had Partner attitude problems and Partner judgement problems. A Partner's judgement is the judgement of the firm as a whole. We, as a Partner group, all agreed that various changes would be brought in. But one Partner undermined it all, soon after we'd started. That showed the staff that we were not for real. If a Partner isn't following the plan, why should I? That isn't fatal, though, provided the Partner's response is positive when it is raised with them. But it uses up a lot of Management's time.

We are looking at the next Partners coming through – we need them to be keen, with a willingness to adapt, with a collaborative leadership style, a willingness to learn "management" ways, and a desire to make a difference. We need to see a desire to build the business, not to protect an empire. A lot of our Partners think that "business" is below them.

They don't realise that "management" is a "thing" that can really benefit a business – and that they might not have what we need. A good biller doesn't make a good Partner. We wouldn't bring any Partner in from outside the firm – we wouldn't know them well enough. There's more to being "the right fit" than hitting billing targets. They can have "Partner-itis" – and it's contagious. We need to completely trust them as they're attached to our name. They are an ambassador for the firm.

Non-lawyer Partners have a completely different mindset. They look at the firm as one overall business – there is no "me, me, me". Why do lawyer Partners think they're so great? We've had to knock some down a peg or two. Partners need to have cabinet responsibility for decisions that have been made – not like the Partner who went back to their team and said, 'It's all rubbish but we've got to do it'."

Managing Partner

"Putting the firm ahead of yourself – that's the essence of partnership. We all have personal concerns, and these change over time, but we need to put on our "Partner" hat and look at what's best for the firm and for the business. Our Business Support leaders seem far more able to do this.

Specific things I would say are that Partners need to be themselves and to be authentic. They need to avoid having favourites, and avoid gossiping or criticising people. More widely than that, we still have some "me, me, me" Partners. Of course, the business may need their fee-earning, but do we need them as Partners, and do we need them involved in the management of the firm?

Just as bad as "me, me, me" Partners are "me and my team" Partners who want decisions to be made that aren't in the interests of the whole firm. They also generate criticism of one team by another, which is not what we need.

I can take Partners having faults – we all have faults. It's a refusal to change that I hate. We need Partners to be self-aware, to listen, and to be willing to change if need be. Partners need to be able to show vulnerability, particularly to junior people. It's okay to say, "I've failed", or "It's hard", or "I'm not okay here".

We need Partners to allow others to be the best at something, and we need them to want to make those people even better, even if it means that they leave the Partner behind. Of course, any system of "Partner profit points" might work against this. We need to reward selfless behaviours, not *selfish* behaviours. This is about the long-term future of the business, not about the here-and-now Partners.

In Partner meetings, we very quickly come off the rails, often because a Partner objects to something when they look at it from their own, personal perspective. Of course, Partners should have a voice, but I would invite them to not use that voice on every issue. Pick your battles. When you do then voice opinions, you'll be listened to. Partners need to realise that they can kill a meeting and they can kill progress. Somehow, Partners have a level of arrogance and confidence that every opinion they've got needs to be listened to. And this is contagious, so management of it is crucial.

Once a partnership decision has been taken, there needs to be cabinet responsibility and the Partners need to embrace and live the decision. Having a large number of Partners in my firm, I'm not managing and leading the business – I'm just managing the Partners. I'm not working strategically to take the firm forward.

The potential amongst the Partners is incredible, if only we stopped looking inward and at each other. My Partners are not all proud of each other. They are too competitive and are comparing themselves to the others and looking after themselves. They should look for more positives in their Partners."

Managing Partner

"My non-negotiables are that Partners have to be nice people – kind, approachable, emotionally intelligent. And they need to be someone I trust. "Normal" is not an exciting word, but we use it a lot in this firm when we debrief after interviewing a candidate. It encapsulates all of the above and means they're not odd, and they made us feel at ease.

Next, Partners must lead by example. They need to walk the walk and do what they say they are going to do. They need to throw themselves into the life of our firm – we are a large family. Finally, they have to put the firm first, before their team and before themselves."

Managing Partner

"I only want to be sat around the table with people I trust implicitly. I want people who have sound judgement, and who are seriously reliable. People who'll be there with me when the going gets tough. I want them to have business acumen. I need to see them putting their staff's needs ahead of their own. I need to see them being supportive of our people."

Managing Partner

"On the question of what makes a great Partner, law doesn't come into it. I need Partners who see themselves first and foremost as business people. We don't just want anyone, either; they have to get – and live – our culture and values. No one can behave like an island here.

We need Partners who are empathetic and who have radar – we can't have Partners who just plough on and try to bulldoze people and obstacles out of the way. We have arrived at a position where we are selectively ruthless – we saw that we had to remove people who just don't fit with all of this.

There are often elephants in the room – some people where you have to ask, "How were they ever made Partners?" My regret is not that we got rid of Partners, but how long it took me to get rid of them. A weak Managing Partner is very damaging for a law firm.

"Law" is not important here – "well-organised" is a far better quality for a Partner to have. "Disorganised" is a disaster for a Partner's clients and their people and for the firm. If you are disorganised, you can only ever be reactive; you can never be on the front foot pushing the business forward. And you simply can't fully develop junior lawyers."

Managing Partner

"When I became a Salaried Partner some years ago, I didn't know what I was doing. I didn't know how a law firm worked. When I became Managing Partner, I was dropped into it. There was no handover phase. No preparation. Succession was a shambles, and we're a large firm. I didn't have a bloody clue what I was doing.

The Partners here usually have a bizarre away day once a year. There is no structure to it. Everyone hates it. We either sit in silence or we argue. We needed real change across the firm. But I got nothing back in Partners meetings – no enthusiasm, no support, no ideas, no input. I got lots of nodding heads, but then they'd all go and do something different. Partners are only custodians for the time being – it's not all about "us" and it's not all about "now".

Our Business Support teams have to be valued – it's because of them that our lawyers can get a comfortable ride. Some Partners just don't see that. I'd like them to see a wider picture, and I'd like them to have a more open-minded, can-do, "growth" mindset.

We live and work in a hugely-changed and fast-changing world. It is seriously hard work making the improvements I want to make and that we need to make. I bet all my Partners would bite my hand off if I could take them back to 2020. It's hard looking ahead at the next generation of Partners – I can't see many Partners coming through. There are no obvious candidates.

I think about the business all the time – my kids often say, "Oh, he's drifted off again" when my mind is on the business at home.

My Partners can totally piss me off. All I want are consistent behaviours and practices from them. It causes bottlenecks everywhere. We've got lots of Partners paddling their own canoes, and they've brought people into the firm who are, in turn, paddling their own canoes, too. I'm going to have to keep trying to push my Partners up a hill – they won't be champions of anything I'm trying to do.

The bane of my life is putting plans together and Partners then turning up without reading the plans and

– depending on how they feel on the day – saying "no" to what I can see the business needs."

Managing Partner

"I'm certainly not The Perfect Partner – it doesn't exist. The perfect *team* of Partners can exist, though.

I was a bad Partner before I became Managing Partner. I was a huge biller, but I had too much belief in my own hype. I've mellowed now, and my new skill is bringing about a desired outcome in any given situation.

I've worked with some of my Partners for a long time. Working with new Partners is trickier. I'm brutally honest with my long-term Partners, but I'd never be like that with my newer Partners. It'll be a sad reflection on the firm if I remain as Managing Partner for a long time. I used to avoid recruiting anyone whom I feared was better than me. I have changed. Now, I don't have to be in charge, and I delegate lots of "senior" tasks. I actively want Partners to take things on.

As we've grown, my personal connection with my Partners has loosened, particularly as we bring in lateral hire Partners from other firms.

We can mitigate the risks associated with bringing in Partners as lateral hires as they'll typically be from similar firms to ourselves. The success rate with lateral hire Partners is still very low – commercial lawyers come in and behave like "big shots".

When I move on from being Managing Partner, unless something changes, I won't be passing the role on to anyone I've yet met or seen in the firm. The pool of talent or potential in "management" terms is very shallow. When I ask our Partners about their role in the business, a huge majority describe themselves as managers, but most are just fee-earners.

Getting Partner support and Partner decisions is a battle. I have to operate in advance of meetings and in advance of decisions being made. It takes a long time to move a short way. I secure partial victories, and I come back later to move things on a step further. It is energy-sapping and time-consuming.

My time and energy could be spent on far more positive, proactive things. There is a void in the firm when it comes to the next wave of Partners. I can see more "Partner" and "management" talent lower down in the firm, including in the Business Support team."

Managing Partner

"Several Partners have changed my life. One Partner wanted to really change things for the better in our firm. I liked their vision and their energy and the way they did things. They created opportunities for me. They genuinely cared for the people around them and they genuinely wanted to use the law to help their clients.

We need a mix of people in our large partnership – different skills, different personalities. But there have to be some red lines. The Partners need the freedom within those lines to grow and develop. Having faults is not the problem with Partners – we've all got faults. A failure to accept and address them is the real problem.

The people we are making Partners now are good technical lawyers but they are excited for our business and they have business acumen and energy and drive. They are developing people that are junior to them. We have highly effective Partners who get good financial results, but they are very demanding and they want their team to be treated differently. Their style can alienate people within the firm.

We have had Partners who should never have been Partners – lateral hires mainly.

We used to have regular Partner meetings that went round and round in circles. It was dispiriting. We have gone to the other extreme now and have very few, where Partners receive reports and can ask me questions. Maybe there's too much of them all just nodding now. I make sure we communicate regularly and fully with the Partners. On the back of that, they let me just get on with a lot."

There are some very interesting and important perspectives in those interviews and chats with law firm leaders that reinforce many of the things we have looked at.

I also talked with other people who are in law firms but who are not sat in the hot seat.

Partner

"I can think of a few "nightmare" Partners. Massive egos. We have one who is a great biller who works 7 days a week. They never delegate anything. They're a dreadful manager of people – they send out really shitty emails to their team. We've lost various people along the way because of them. We work around them.

The Partner who changed my life when I was a junior lawyer was one who had time for me and who taught me all that I know. I shared a room with them and every day at 4pm, we'd sit down and they'd invest their time in developing me. Billing is the easy part of being a Partner – the people stuff is the important stuff, but it is far harder."

Partner

"Being a good Partner is all about people. Workaholics don't make great Partners. We've had good lawyers, but they're not always the Partners you want. You need to take junior lawyers with you – give them time, if the firm allows you to give them time. The really important "people" things are not explored in interviews. Lateral hires can therefore cause problems.

There are so many drains on your time when you are a Partner. Partners meetings can be stressful and confrontational.

If you delegate a job to someone, it is your responsibility to make sure they are armed to do the job, including by you. It makes business sense, too. Money is not the only measure of success.

The best Partner I had when I was a junior lawyer was a very good lawyer but was also very calm and they always had an open door. The worst Partner I worked with was rude, and would fly off the handle. They were impatient and unapproachable. They were the reason I left that firm. You don't have to actually like the Partner but I didn't respect or trust them either. We lost an awful lot of good and senior people because of them. How was that allowed to continue?"

Partner

"You only really know if you've got the right Partners when a crisis arises – and it's too late then. Partners are all charming at the start. Beware who you let in, though! A bad Partner can wreck so much.

Partners may have different needs in their personal lives – their personal needs need to come second to those of the firm. They need to keep their personal lives in order as these can impact on the firm.

A Partner's main objective needs to be "What's best for the business?" and not "How do I feel today?"

Law firms rely on their reputation and their integrity. We had a Partner who was simply unethical. We are Officers of the Court; we have to be totally honest and professional. Someone being completely honest makes up for all sorts of other shortcomings on their part. And they're not *your* clients, even if you brought them in – they're the firm's clients.

Partners can block people rising – they should lift them up instead. That is a great legacy. Partners can take credit, but instead they need to give credit. Are we even all on the same side? Openness on the part of all Partners should be non-negotiable. Partner personalities are hard work – if you add in secretiveness, it becomes debilitating.

I'd move very slowly if I was putting a partnership together now. If you get it wrong, you need to correct it quickly. Partners are responsible for the standing in the country of the legal profession. Within the firm, the Partners are our policemen, but they need to accept that policemen need to be policed, too."

Senior Business Support

"We need business efficiency. Our Partners don't push efficiency though – we have to push them.

I wouldn't be where I am now without Partners in the past who gave me opportunities and encouragement. One particular Partner really made me great – they were superb at communication and collaboration. Even now, I still try to emulate them.

Everything would be easy in our law firm if it wasn't for the Partners. The Partners each want to do everything their way. They bend the rules to suit them. We spend ages as the Business Support team trying to arrive at a common way of doing things across the firm. We'll never achieve that.

Partners are always concerned with why someone else is being paid what they're being paid. They always want special treatment for their own team. There is "them" and "us" between different teams.

Partners need to accept that we are in this business – indeed, that we're in business – together. We're on the same side – they don't need to feel that Business Support is working against them. Lower your defences and work with us!

We have had a high-billing Partner who was rude – a bully. Junior lawyers would be in tears.

Partners might not realise that the pressures of legal work and of partnership can change their personality. Partners don't like change – they ask us to never change the IT system again. That tells you something that is not good… IT improvements are coming all the time, and the pace of change is accelerating.

If I could wave a wand, I would ensure that amongst Partners there was no short-term thinking, and I'd focus on developing all our staff in all parts of the firm, as the money will follow.

The Perfect Partner is very much not the highest biller or the hardest worker or even the best lawyer. Rather, the Perfect Partner is a good and strong role model who embraces the idea of other people going beyond them."

Senior Business Support

"Yes, it's important for Partners to bring in business and to earn fees, but they need to care – to care about the business and to care about effecting change. A Partner should not be an outlier just going through the motions and performing a role.

They usually get partnership because they generate good fees. We need far more than that from Partners. Lawyers like to talk. They talk a good game, but they don't walk the walk.

We have a core group of Partners in my firm who do everything – the rest are just functionaries. "Partner" is an old-fashioned concept – they need to be "business leaders". Not enough Partners see themselves as that. We need Partners who are willing to challenge the status quo, who have the humility to be wrong, who don't have big egos, who don't insist on having a say on everything, and who say, "Fuck it – let's try it". Lawyers typically don't do these things.

Progress is better than perfection; progress is better than point-scoring. We need to actually do things, or we'll suffer from planning fatigue. A firm has to invest in its Partners – you rise to "Partner", but you don't necessarily lead and inspire.

Partners don't listen. They never ask, "What does the business need from me?" And someone who speaks to junior people in a way that is different to how they speak to senior people is terrible.

It is not a Partner's responsibility to always make the right decisions. It *is* a Partner's responsibility, though, to allow decisions to be made. A Partner needs to ask themselves, "Am I helping a sensible decision to be made here, or am I just giving my opinion and thus de-railing the decision-making process?"

I can see the Partners of the future at my firm. They really care and they are not satisfied with how things are – they want to make things better. A lot of our fee-earners are simply not Partner material. As Partners, we are all tarred with the same brush.

When a Partner comes in from another firm, there can be a culture clash. Don't assume it will work out! We have seen Partners come in and decimate teams. They were bullies.

We need to be able to trust every Partner – trust them to do the right thing, including when no one is looking. It's hard to trust a Partner if you don't know them."

Senior Business Support

"First and foremost, a Partner needs to be in business. A Partner needs to be a professional, who cares about people, and who is profitable. A helpful Partner listens to my input and learns from it. An unhelpful one appears to listen, agrees with me, and then does nothing. They just nod so that they can carry on doing things the same old way. The best Partners argue with me, we reach agreement, and then they do what we've agreed.

I have worked with some amazing Partners, for example on pitches for new business. I saw that where the lead Partner allowed their team to engage directly with the potential client, without that Partner being involved, we always won that pitch. The team rose and were amazing and the clients could see that we operated as a team and that the whole team would be there for them – it wasn't all about the Partner. The Partner trusted the team and made them feel good. They reached new heights, and the business was the ultimate winner.

A law firm can never move faster than the most risk-averse, most-uncommercial, and most-argumentative Partner. The best Partners have balance – they are not extraordinary in any one aspect. And when they show respect, they get respect back."

Junior Lawyer

"The worst Partner experience I had was with a Partner who utterly dismissed my expertise and input. It wasn't done in a rational way – it was based on a desire to win any argument at any cost, even with a junior lawyer who was helping them. It knocked the stuffing out of me, and out of others. Junior people got destroyed. It stopped us thinking for ourselves. You can't do anything about it because they're a Partner. No one stood up for us."

Junior Lawyer

"I value regular feedback from Partners – don't keep me in the dark as to how I'm doing! Respect for a Partner comes from their calmness. One Partner was so rude and demanding that I saw the other Partners doing V-signs behind their back, in front of junior people. Another Partner was a genius, but he stressed everyone out and never explained jobs he wanted junior lawyers to do for them. Lawyers left the firm, again and again.

The other Partners respected them for their fees and turned a blind eye to the revolving door they were causing. People had breakdowns because of them. The core is respect – you earn respect; you don't just demand and get it.

If something goes wrong, the Partner needs to step up and be calm. Have the junior's back. Sitting in front of a Partner while they signed your post each day was the chance to talk – that's gone and we should get it back.

Some Partners walk the floor. Others don't – they think they're too busy for that. It's that day-to-day contact that makes the difference. One Partner I work with doesn't know I exist – they never say hello to me. When Partners come from other offices, they don't say hello.

I once took a day off to accompany a friend to her appointment at hospital. I explained this, but the Partner made me work all day even though I'd booked a day's holiday. And I was sent an 80-page document to work through by a Partner whilst I was off work recovering from an operation. I have seen a Partner ask a heavily pregnant lady to carry a full box of files. Some Partners are inhumane, completely lacking self-awareness. They should remain as senior lawyers, not be made Partners.

We have a clear set of criteria for internal Partner promotions, but what about lateral hires? Partnership is and should be seen as a burden. It's not a walk in the park. It is a responsibility. Look at everyone around you – you are responsible for them and their families. Don't be self-obsessed.

A bad Partner costs a firm time and money. I'd go further and say that it costs the firm its good name too, and its soul. People leave Partners, not the firm. Partners should ask juniors – what can I do to help you?

A Partner's team is made of humans, not machines. Don't make them feel like being human is a failure – being human is not a failure. Taking holidays is a strength, not a weakness. Partners dictate the culture of a firm. They should draw the lines and they should police decency. Being a Partner isn't about law, it's about people."

Junior Lawyer

"Stories about Partners spread like wildfire. Good stories, but more so bad stories. Everyone knows.

And not just in the office – have a look at the website called Roll On Friday. In my firm, we have seen Partners outright shouting at junior people, including publicly.

And because it's a Partner, there was no one the junior person could take it to. It destroys the whole vibe in the firm. It's bullying.

I have seen a Partner literally screaming and cursing at one of the Business Support team. That was bad, but not as bad as the fact that nothing happened to them as a result. It creates a horrible atmosphere.

I can see no future with my current firm – they have no plans for me."

Junior Lawyer

"I have seen a Partner throw a textbook, in anger, at another junior lawyer sat on the other side of the room, and then storm into their room and slam the door shut."

Junior Lawyer

"A Partner stood over me shouting. They didn't stop even when I burst into tears."

Senior Lawyer

"One Partner created a toxic environment. A total dictator. Everyone had to do everything their way. They had no respect for people's holidays, for example. They literally demanded that people respect them. If you have to demand it, it's not happening. They wanted to sack people for the smallest things. They felt like they owned us. Lots of senior, talented people left the firm. And other fee-earners followed them out the door."

Junior Lawyer

"The worst Partner I worked under resorted to personal insults, and he was never taken to task over this by Management. I have seen Partners who jump up and down, who don't listen, and who kick off. It's all about 'me, me, me'."

Junior Lawyer

"The worst Partner for me was a Partner who kept promising things. We all realised they never kept promises and were just manipulating us.

I'm yet to find a Partner who can do all that is needed from them – law, billing, BD, and management. Small things count. Yes, be a good lawyer and work hard.

Managerially, though, I think some Partners do it in a tick-box, scorecard way. I'd focus on the fact that people learn in different ways. Focus on the person in front of you. Your way of learning may not be their way of learning. All these people are the future of the firm. Partner behaviours dictate whether a junior lawyer will want to stay at a firm."

Senior Business Support

"The best Partner ever was the most influential Partner ever – Dave. He had a saying – "Pass it on". He always wanted to develop other people. He unhesitatingly gave me time as an individual. He was a very good listener and a great teacher.

He saw delegation as a teaching opportunity. He trusted me – he never micromanaged. He made me look at things from the perspective of others."

Junior Lawyer

"The best Partner ever? One Partner I worked with had a huge brain, and they were very approachable. They were always willing to give me time, to share, and to delegate. They involved me. No drama, no unloading on me, no causing stress to other people. They invested time with me at the start of every delegated task. Partners should guide you and explain what and why."

Junior Lawyer

"One Partner I worked with was amazing. Brilliant. The most conscientious and considerate person I've ever worked with. They never put themselves first. They never expected the buck to stop at a junior lawyer's desk. They commanded so much respect. We wanted to do everything we could for them. They never lost staff. There was a queue of lawyers wanting to work for them, because news about you travels fast when you're a great Partner."

So, those are some of the discussions I have had with people in law firms which relate directly to the question of what makes a good and a bad Partner. You can clearly see some Leadership Behaviours in there, and some of the "bad" behaviours we listed.

I'd like to finish this chapter by highlighting what I thought were some other dynamite comments from the interviews, all of these coming from junior lawyers. I felt these were particularly powerful statements:

- "The law is the last thing that is important here."

- "Partners should think of the firm in five or ten years' time, whether or not they're going to still be in it."

- "As the generations change, the gulf between Partners and juniors is widening – it's getting deeper and wider every year."

- "You're writing a very important book here, Simon – I hope it gets into the hands of Partners and gives them food for thought."

CHAPTER 18

LEADERSHIP ACTION: MOVING ALONG THE RAILS

Having led a successful brainstorm and arrived at a set of team rails, "all talk and no action" kills ambition within a team and that – in turn – extinguishes leadership. We now need to get moving along those rails, rather than just sitting motionless on them. We need to hear a new sound, the sound of a train's wheels trundling along a track. It's time to bring in the next Leadership Action.

We mustn't forget, though, that people are busy. Clients are calling. Lawyers' heads are full. This needs accommodating and nurturing by the leader. And I don't just mean getting things moving at the start. I mean, keeping things moving after that. "Flashes in the pan" kill ambition and kill leadership.

The leader needs to accept and factor into their plans and actions the fact that some of this is going to become monotonous and even downright boring! The leader needs to keep the faith and encourage the team to keep the faith. "This is what we do. When we examined ourselves, we saw how best we can do it – so let's stick to our guns and stay on the rails". What the leader, in effect, is saying is, "This may become repetitious and dull, but big pay rises and bonuses and promotions are anything but!"

The team has identified the rails during the brainstorm. To get and keep things moving, the Leadership Actions that are needed next flow directly from the Leadership Behaviours we have looked at:

- Involve everyone. Delegate parts of the plan and responsibility for particular rails to team members. Then let them get on with it

- Don't micromanage. Let people make mistakes, fail, and learn

- Communications – give feedback to the team on how things are going

- Celebrate successes and failures

- Let everyone know this isn't going to be going away – fix a series of monthly "Review and Boost" meetings now – we all love a bit of R&B!

- Give credit – not just for successes but for effort

- At the R&B meetings, get all those who had tasks delegated to them to report to the team. The leader does very little talking!

- Set targets along the way and celebrate hitting them

- Lead by example

- Do what you said you were going to do

- Make sure Leadership Behaviours are exhibited by everyone in the team – no group of individuals is going to perform as a team if there is no universal trust and respect between them

- Raise accountability levels – is everyone doing what the plan needs them to do, and what they said they'll do?

This last bullet point needs dwelling on as we are talking about law firms here. A curious difference between this larger "team" example and the earlier example we looked at – of a single Partner who works on cases with a junior lawyer or lawyers – is that the leader may have *other Partners* in the team here.

These other Partners are not the leader of the group or team in this instance. However, this project absolutely needs them all to lead by example when it comes to the rails and to exhibit the Leadership Behaviours that are by now familiar to us.

Where things break down in this scenario is where the team's leader tries to do things, but other *Partners* in the team go their own way, or they do things the way they have always done them, because they are Partners. Or, worse, they sabotage (directly or indirectly by their contrary behaviours) what the leader is trying to achieve with the team. Not all saboteurs wear masks.

This could be borne out of a mindset where, "I'm a Partner – no one's telling me how to do my job", or it might less damagingly be because the Partner's head is full and they're too busy to take new things on board. Either way, their contrary or disparate behaviours can show the team that there is one rule for one and one rule for everyone else. This is a situation that must be addressed by the leader. If it isn't addressed, there will be a loud popping noise before long.

Partners have to be team members, too, and support the team's leader as they work to keep the team on the rails and move them along those rails.

They need to put their own views and interests behind those of the team. Any Partner not doing so literally spoils the chances of the team realising their ambitions and enjoying the rewards that inevitably go with that. A Partner being recalcitrant (or horrible) is being extremely selfish and damaging. They are literally holding back the opportunity for a group of people – often young people – to do better in life.

Leadership Actions thus keep things on the rails and move the team forward along the rails. By way of a structured programme of Review & Boost meetings, where the leader has the courage to embrace what might (at times) feel like monotony, the team's sights and energy levels are raised and are continuously focused on the main events, not on new shiny things. The regular R&B meetings are supplemented by ongoing ad hoc communications within the team, and the six-monthly individual appraisals with the Team Leader become the R&B meeting par excellence.

Not everything that is required here can be delivered by the leader alone, or even by the Partners who are local to this team. The firm as a whole has a key role to play. The leader and the Partners in the team might well exhibit all the right Leadership Behaviours (such as a desire to develop the people in the team and to ensure career progression and reward and opportunities for those who help the team move along the rails). But if

Senior Management is looking for different things from the lawyers, or there is a career path that rewards different behaviours, or there is an inconsistent application of policies and benefits across the firm, guess what noise you'll hear?

What is therefore required, of course, is the ultimate leader of the firm to bring all the Partners together, to help them to become leaders, and to arrive with them at the key things that the business needs each part of the business to deliver on. The Partner group (which is now hopefully the leadership group) then have to be given the tools and the right structures and resources. This enables them to demonstrate to their respective team members that they are not talking hot air but rather that they have the firm behind them and that they are able to bring an arsenal to bear on the individuals' and the team's well-being, reward, and development – if the right things are done in the right way.

There needs to be consistency across every part and every level in the firm, so that lawyers, Partners, and Business Support teams are all doing things the right way and the same way. Everyone in the firm has to be treated the same way for this to work.

It is fatal if one Partner and one team can be a law unto themselves. It is fatal, here, if your prospects of progression in a firm depend on which Partner you work with.

It is also fatal if the team's leader asks a lawyer to deliver X, but the firm then rewards others for doing Y. Fairness, transparency, and consistency are all Leadership Behaviours.

I should add that Partners do not have a monopoly on "leadership" in a law firm. As we've discussed, one Leadership Action is to inculcate Leadership Behaviours across the team. Not only does this oil the wheels of teamwork, it also nurtures the next generation of leaders (or it shines a light on junior individuals whose leadership skills might be of real value to the business even now). It's the job of every leader to create the next leader – and to create leaders generally. There is no greater success for leaders than more leaders!

I have seen many situations where the Partner is the boss, but someone more junior in the team is, in fact, the leader, as a result of their respective bad and good behaviours. I always think it a great sign of a Partner, particularly of an Equity Partner, where they open the door to themselves and the team being led by someone more junior – by someone who has the right and better skills. It is a right-thinking Partner who buries all concerns of vanity or perception to put the team and the business first. And it is a right-thinking law firm that encourages and rewards and invests in burgeoning leadership traits and skills in its junior people.

Every Partner has a selfless role in, and responsibility for, policing these Leadership Behaviours and these rails. A Partner personally having their team behave in different ways with different rules, or a Partner pressing for special treatment for their whole team or someone in it, all undermine the foundations for growth that we are trying to build here. We will never reach the stars without *every* Partner behaving as a leader and embracing and moving along the selected rails.

Where this amazing state of affairs is achieved, the Partners can truly boast of success. Their sustained adherence to the chosen rails will have secured them a truly glittering prize. That is, together, they will have built a way – the firm's way – of doing things.

CHAPTER 19

THE WAY TO THE STARS

Where you have (a) all the Partners in a firm universally exhibiting Leadership Behaviours, and (b) all the Partners and their people moving along selected rails as a result of team efforts flowing from Leadership Actions, and (c) where those rails incorporate all aspects needed to strengthen the four legs of the stool and to move the firm along The Money Journey, it all takes a firm to a very special place. But the place is not what or where lawyers might have expected all of this to go.

I have frequently been pressed by lawyers in firms that I have worked with to define – in some exciting and exact physical terms – precisely the destination that our joint efforts will be taking them to. As I have said elsewhere in this book, though, this is not a journey where we take off and then land somewhere. It is not a finite journey. It is a "forever" journey, but it will be very comfortable (as there is no turbulence in space), and it will be extremely enjoyable, which team environments, personal development, pay rises, promotions, and bonuses usually are.

This lack of a defined, limited destination is very different to what you see in the strategies that some law firms boast of, where the destination is, for example,

"To be the leading law firm in the region, in business law, with seven new PLC clients and an increase in turnover of 20% per year".

Here, whilst we very much aim to get somewhere special, that "somewhere special" is not a place. It is a *way*.

The desired and very desirable destination on our journey is the arrival by a firm at a way (*its* way) of doing things. It is a way that is *the only way* that the firm does things. It is a way that everyone in the firm – *that is, absolutely everyone* – embraces and embodies.

The destination is a way which has four component parts:

Our Way – Internal:

1. How we look after our people, and what we need from them

2. How we operate as a business, and one that is regulated

Our Way – External:

3. How we look after our clients, and what we need from them

4. How we look after our communities

Hopefully, you will immediately see that everything that I have been talking about in this book – and in my other books – converges here to give a law firm its way… *The Perfect Way*. You can see how it all comes together at this point. The rails all take us towards a way:

- How do we look after our people? Look no further than Leadership Behaviours!

- How do we operate as a business? Look no further than The Money Journey!

- How do we discharge the responsibilities that come with us being regulated? Partners leading by example to strengthen the Compliance leg of the stool!

- How do we look after our clients? See the Service Pledge, the cross-caring, and the proactive care we have looked at

The fourth part of The Perfect Way is "How we look after our communities." Your way might include a commitment to put something back into the communities in which you operate, or into some other communities.

At my firm, we supported various communities and causes. Most excitingly, we came together as a team to help fund the building of a hospital, orphanage, and school in India, a project in which one of our people was personally involved.

It's not for me to say any firm should do these things. It is for me, however, to say that such works are incredibly uplifting and are very good for the spirit of the team that you are relying on to drive your business forward. They are also simply downright good things to do.

Looking at the parts of The Perfect Way, you will see that everything overlaps and dovetails nicely together – the Leadership Behaviours, the four legs of the stool,

The Money Journey, and client care. Having a way is truly the glittering prize. All four legs of the stool are continually strengthened.

The ultimate owners of, and evangelists about, your way should be the Partners in the firm, of course.

In short (and again, these are not my words, but I love them and have adapted them), every Partner must be a leader who:

- Knows The Way
- Shows The Way
- Goes The Way

The elements of your way need to permeate every facet of the law firm; everything it does internally and externally, including:

- The behaviours that will be encouraged and tolerated at all levels
- The service the firm delivers to clients
- Its approach to care for clients has to be far wider than just dealing with their case
- All the firm's messaging and marketing
- Its appraisal and review structures, at every level
- Its approach to reward and career progression
- The agendas of every team, office, and Partner meeting
- Every quarterly or annual all-staff meeting
- All Learning and Development programmes

Your rails, and your Partners' ownership of them, will achieve this.

With all of this in place, we are now very close to blast off! We have the rocket fuel that we need. We just need some... concrete.

CHAPTER 20

HOT AIR OR CONCRETE?

Key to all that we are looking at is one of the over-arching things that I did right during my time as a Managing Partner, and that I now work very hard with law firms to help them achieve. That is, my preference for concrete as opposed to hot air.

I don't recommend you do this, but have you ever spent hours browsing law firms' websites? I have. They are peppered with vacuous statements, which – from professional organisations whose tools of the trade are words themselves – often leave me open-mouthed and scratching my head.

What do they promise to clients?

- "We are different"
- "We are unique"
- "We do law differently",
- "We're unlike any other law firm"
- "We are professional"
- "We are expert"
- "Not your ordinary law firm"
- "We are client-centric"

- "We are client-focused"
- "We put you, the client, at the centre of everything we do"
- "Award-winning"
- "Client excellence" [I don't know what that one means]
- "We are a leading law firm"
- "Our clients take priority"
- "We take the time to understand your needs"

I could go on.

What do they promise to potential employees?

- "A modern workplace"
- "We maximise your potential"
- "A collaborative and supportive environment"
- "A happy, dedicated team"
- "A rewarding long-lasting career"

Again, I could go on.

These are just words. They do not withstand any scrutiny at all. All you'd have to say in response to see the house of cards crumble is, "Okay then – prove it". They are hot air. They have probably been written by an internal or external marketing executive and signed off by a Partner who likes the sound of them.

These words make eyes roll, not light up.

One pound of concrete trumps warehouses full of hot air. In every aspect of your way and The Money

Journey, you should strive to have something tangible and meaningful in place. Mean what you say and do what you say. Clients (and future clients) will value it, and your people (and future people) will value, respect, and respond to it.

I also believe it will help the business to secure, for the long term, all the inputs and behaviours it needs that will benefit it, all the people in it, and all the people who are served by it. It actually supports the rise of, and the continuance of, your way. Concrete holds rails in place; hot air doesn't.

I have worked through this book and have pulled together what I see as the significant opportunities for a firm to stand out from the usual hot air factories that surround them in the legal sector by having structures and institutions and tangible cornerstones that show that the firm means – in every sense of the word – business.

These are, of course, just the opportunities I see to secure more credibility, buy-in, and progress. In all your dimensions, you might be able to challenge loose concepts or ideas and identify areas where you could pour some good concrete.

Here are the opportunities that I see for concrete to be poured:

Hot air	Concrete
A great culture / a great environment / a great place to work	Our Partners are required to exhibit Leadership Behaviours – a non-negotiable. We recognise

Hot air	Concrete
	Leadership Behaviours (or lack thereof) in Partner reward mechanisms. Across the whole firm, there is a clear intolerance of contrary behaviours, attitudes, and performance – action will be taken
Exciting career opportunities	We have a clear and fair career path and appraisal programme, that rewards the right things
We will invest in your development	We have an Academy, with a tailored programme and plan for each person – including the development of Leadership Behaviours at all levels
We offer our clients a great service	We all work to a Service Pledge that we all designed
We care for our clients	You come into the centre of our firm, not into one team or onto one desk. No "my client" is allowed here

Hot air	Concrete
We care for our clients	We extend proactive care (using the Platforms that I mention in this book) to help clients avoid trauma and expense down the line and to reduce their legal bills
We are different / we're unlike other law firms	Our differentiators are concrete – our Service Pledge, our all-round care, and our proactive care
We're a well-run business	To make our business sustainable and to enable us to touch more lives, The Money Journey is followed by every team here, with a focus on team Gross Margins and cash. Our Partners are developed as leaders. We have Review & Booster meetings across the teams to make sure we remain on our chosen rails so we never forget the four legs of the stool and The Money Journey
We are one big, happy team	Everyone here does everything our way, and we constantly provide

Hot air	Concrete
	training to all our existing and new people on all aspects of it, via our Academy

Let's have a closer look at that last point – the Academy.

CHAPTER 21

THE ACADEMY

Every law firm delivers training to its people. It might be anti-money laundering training, IT training, training to stop cyber-attacks, or training to help a person or a group of people to be better in their particular roles within the firm, whether that be a legal role or a Business Support role. These are all good, but there's no need for it all to sound so formal and "routine".

You could make it much more engaging. You could move it away from being a process into something a lot more uplifting. You could make it a "thing" – a piece of concrete – and as such, it could be a much more compelling dimension to your Employer Brand. In terms of attracting new talent, which will frankly be spoiled for choice "out there", it could strengthen your proposition.

What I am talking about here goes much, much further than firms typically go, because of course, the law firm and the legal business that I am advocating will have long since left other, normal "firms of solicitors" in its wake as it journeys to the stars.

What I am talking about here is not just a way of providing the training that you were always going to be providing. What I am talking about here is a fundamental part of the whole Moon and stars project. It is a way of ensuring the maintenance at the heart of a law firm of its adherence to its rails and, thus, its *way* of doing things, both internally and externally. In fact, without the organ I describe here, it would be very hard to ensure the longevity and purity of your way.

Think about the aspects of a law firm that we have examined and strengthened on our journey over my three books to arrive at a perfect legal business that is manned by perfect lawyers, all of whom are led by Perfect Partners. Now you can see the huge range of training opportunities and needs that a firm needs if it is to secure delivery of all those aspects.

Unlike regular firms of solicitors who, in my experience, are past masters at getting bored easily and moving from new thing to new thing, The Perfect Legal Business doesn't do "flash in the pan".

Rather, it recognises that daily pressures can distract focus and it constantly works to keep the rails and the firm's way at the forefront of everyone's minds. It does this by bringing these aspects into an ongoing training regime – its Academy.

I mentioned earlier that lawyers' heads are literally full – and so are those of the busy Business Support team – so it is genuinely hard for them all to embed and embrace new disciplines and practices. Throwing a bucket of water at the challenge won't get you far, therefore. A sustained drip, drip, drip, though? Now that's different – that consistency can erode granite. What we need instead of various ad hoc events being laid on to ensure that people are getting all the obligatory training they need, as well as some developmental training, is a training curriculum and institution that meets a range of needs:

- It needs to help everyone to be involved in all compliance and risk management efforts

- It needs to help everyone to be good at their current jobs

- It needs to get everyone ready for their next jobs in the firm

- It needs to reinforce and catalyse every aspect of The Money Journey

- It needs to promote and reinforce all aspects of the Leadership Behaviours – at all levels

- It needs to promote and reinforce, for the long term, all the rails and, thus, all aspects of the firm's way

By the last point, I mean that everyone in the firm constantly undergoes training and development in:

- Internal aspects of our way – the rails that govern how we look after our people, our culture, and how we operate as a regulated, profit-rich, cash-rich, growing business

- External aspects of our way – the rails that govern how we treat and develop and care for our clients, and how we give back to our communities and to society

Everyone in the firm needs to be a student at this Academy. That is from the Managing Partner across the entire firm. That obviously includes all Partners. Ideally, Partners will be amongst the tutors at the Academy.

And everyone is a student at the Academy from the moment they arrive at the firm until the moment they leave. There is an accelerated module to bring lateral hires and new employees into the way, so that the induction process runs deep and is the early point at which the rails – and, thus, the way – are safeguarded.

You can see that this is not an institution that ticks boxes. Nor is it a reactive organisation that just does reminders or top-ups. Rather, it is a central force that helps to make the law firm a perfect legal business, with perfect lawyers led by Perfect Partners.

If you go back to the Leadership Behaviours, you can see how the Academy, with the curriculum I am setting out, can deliver and reinforce so many of the good leadership behaviours listed there. Not least of all, it can show everyone in the firm that there is a *plan for them* and that the firm is keen to develop them for their own benefit and for the benefit of the business.

That is light years away from people getting an email saying, "You are required to attend the next obligatory anti-money laundering training session". Now, the language and the spirit around such things are far more positive – "Let's keep what we've built here safe!"

The programme can't last without the Academy. Think back to all the initiatives you might have seen in a law firm over the years – where are they now? The difference is consistency. Drip, drip, drip – sticking to the rails rather than looking for something new all the time.

Key to the Leadership Behaviours we have looked at, and a key part of the cement that binds good people to a firm (if you'll excuse the pun), is them seeing something concrete that directly benefits them, such as the firm having a plan and an Academy for them. How amazing must that feel?

The Academy is part of that in any event, but as well as the "consistency" I just mentioned, a fundamental need in all of this is for everything to be joined together. A cog turning on its own gets nothing anywhere. Hence, the Academy goes hand in hand with a tailored, transparent, fair career path that rewards the right hard and soft behaviours. And it goes hand in hand with a committed appraisal process where people get detailed, honest feedback on an ongoing basis.

I set academies up as part of my Perfect Legal Business programme with law firms. A firm's imagination can run wild when the academies are being set up and the curriculum is being designed. Things get really enjoyable when we talk about Fresher's Week and the end-of-term prom!

The launch and success of an Academy depends on the Partners in the firm exhibiting Leadership Behaviours and recognising its importance. It also depends on them recognising the importance of delivering an associated, active, and meaningful appraisal process to a firm's people and the value of both of these elements in the short, medium, and long terms to the business. Everything fits together.

You can see the vital role of Partners in this dimension, too. If there is no Partner engagement, there can be no Academy, and a firm cannot then have its way of doing everything. Just some Partners getting involved is the same as no Partners getting involved.

Across a partnership, in terms of the Academy, but also in terms of all the themes we have looked at in this book, there will typically be a range of Partner responses and a range of levels of belief and engagement. Let's look at the different types of Partner that my model throws up.

CHAPTER 22

WHAT TYPE OF PARTNER ARE YOU IN THIS MODEL?

You can now see the behaviours and contributions that I believe a law firm, its business and its people need to see in the firm's Partners if the firm is to grow sustainably in all the right ways.

My model of The Perfect Legal Business, The Perfect Lawyer, and now The Perfect Partner, requires certain traits, behaviours, and contributions from a law firm's Partners. If you at all agree that there is something in this model, then you might find it an interesting exercise to assess what Partner types are currently present in your law firm against my criteria, and to assess whether they are helping or hindering progress.

You might also be unable to resist assessing what Partner type you are, or – if you are not yet a Partner – what Partner type you aspire to be.

This isn't a science, of course. The criteria I use and the categories I have arrived at below, are based on hard business lessons but also on feelings. When you are dealing with *people*, as we very much are in law firms, feelings are important. Watch what happens if you ignore feelings. People stay at firms, or join firms, or go the extra mile for firms, based on their feelings.

So, it's not a science, but I believe that there are general groupings that Partners can fall into within my model. It would be impossible, though, to simply divide Partners up into Type A or Type B, for example. There are a huge number of nuances and overlaps. Law firms and partnerships are broad churches and are the better for being so – provided that the decision-making process is not paralysed and provided that there are some rails and some red lines in place.

Many firms do, of course, already try to assess and score their Partners. Some of the "balanced scorecard" and other complex Partner review systems that I have seen in operation can indeed help to build some of the qualities that a business needs in its Partners.

The more complex the system, however, the more time the process takes each year, and the more time the Partners spend behind closed doors with each other dissecting their scores and venting their anger at the scores (and often the ensuing rewards) given to others.

Additionally, many of the "scorecard" systems don't sufficiently factor in (or give sufficient weight to) the very human elements that I believe are required of Partners, which are the very elements that shine so brightly in this book. "Feelings" don't come across well on a piece of paper.

As you'll see in my conclusions below, I believe that better people make better Partners, not bigger billers.

Unlike many Partner review and scoring systems, my categories don't involve looking at a Partner's financial numbers in detail. Of course, I do look at what a Partner's core contribution to the business is, as a partnership made up of solely nice people isn't going to get far.

My Partner categories take into account my belief that if you can get your whole Partner group on the same, good rails, and all pushing and pulling the firm along those rails, then the direct and indirect benefits for the business are huge. They can transcend anything that individual Partners can do in terms of chargeable hours and billings.

Obliging a Partner to focus on their own personal numbers will make the firm a bit of money, but as a consequence I believe the firm will miss out on a fortune and on a much brighter future.

Therefore, my categories look at whether a Partner helps the firm to identify and then adhere to a set of rails and thus build and maintain the firm's *way* and its two internal aspects (Colleagues and Cash) and its two external aspects (Clients and Community).

If they behave as leaders who help to build and maintain the rails that give a firm its way, they are an asset indeed. If they don't, they are slowing the firm down, regardless of how much they bill. Even with their billing, they will be holding the firm – and the progress of all the people in it – back.

Yes, a Partner's hard contribution to the business needs to be visible. That's not enough, though, as that just keeps a firm where it is. The real value in a Partner is where they are helping to take the firm. Are they taking it forward? Backwards? To the Moon and the stars?

This all points towards there being a number of broad categories of Partner within a law firm that has aspirations to become The Perfect Legal Business:

The Roadblock

These Partners do not see themselves as accountable to the firm and/or they do not exhibit Leadership Behaviours (and might even exhibit toxic behaviours), and/or they do not embrace the team's rails or the various aspects of The Money Journey. Rather, they do things their way – the way they've always done things. And they feel that as a Partner and therefore as a boss, they need to be heard.

By de-railing the team's or the firm's decision-making processes, they prevent other Partners from taking effective Leadership Actions, and they prevent progress in general. They think only of themselves, not of the team or the whole firm or of the other people in either. They prevent the team and the firm from moving forward along a set of rails as one. They both, therefore, move backwards. They are not positive influencers and do not lead by example.

Key features of the Roadblock can include some or all of the following:

- They weaken some or all of the four legs of the stool – Clients (by giving poor service), Colleagues (by being horrible), Compliance (by treating compliance with the rules as not applying to them), and Cash (by charging favoured clients low fees and by having a string of unpaid bills on their books)

- They behave like a boss, not as a leader – they feel like they're important, and certainly more important than people "below" them

- They see clients as "my client", and no one else is allowed to interact with those clients

- They can't see the value in building a firm's way – they only respect their own way

Roadblocks feel duty-bound to oppose things, even minutiae, which cripples the decision-making process in general and prevents the construction of rails and uplifting team plans.

A Partner doesn't have to be guilty of all of these traits to fall into the Roadblock category. Any one of them will be damaging to the firm.

Hopefully, in any firm, Roadblocks are small in number. They need to be zero in number.

The Coiled Spring

In any law firm, Coiled Springs – that is, Partners who are full of potential to be The Perfect Partner given the right guidance, environment, and incentives – can be high in number or high as a percentage of the overall partnership. They are the mainstay of many firms: good, reliable, steady Partners who accept that they are answerable to the firm and its Management, and who do not exhibit any toxic behaviours. They have no bad impact and actually have some good impact as they exhibit some of the easier, more general Leadership Behaviours. They don't have intrusive tendencies and might sit quietly in Partner meetings rather than getting involved in minutiae that have no real impact on their work.

To some degree, they work locally within a firm. They do a good job for their clients and they work well with one or more junior lawyers, but they don't actively push forward any initiatives more widely than that. Where they are fee-earners, they don't fully follow the letter or the spirit of The Money Journey, but then again, they don't need to, as they can hit their billing target without all of that. They are good fee-earners who try to hit their billing target each year or do a good job in one of the Business Support teams rather than really contributing like business owners, business pushers, or business changers.

Often, they are like this because that's what the firm has made them into, and because that is all that the firm requires from them. Their only involvement is as a fee-earner and their reward is based on them hitting their annual billing target.

They keep a firm going around its traditional orbit. They are not the people to help a firm to shoot for the stars. Not yet, that is.

The potential within the Coiled Springs group is vast. Their fee-earning won't change anything, but if we can unlock their energy and if we can get them to become Accelerators – see below – the benefits for the business would be enormous.

That potential cannot be unlocked, though, unless the firm asks for something different from them and encourages them to provide a different input to the business.

They need to be invited into a central discussion around the future of the firm they are Partners in, and they need to be part of a high-level brainstorm led by the firm's Senior Management Team. What works for teams works for the partnership itself. A partnership brainstorm and planning and prioritising session that has the four legs of the stool, the laying of rails, and the building of its way at its heart (instead of the unfocused subject matter that is sometimes central to Partner "Strategy" days or "Awaydays") will identify the rails that the firm needs to lay down and will clarify the inputs that all Partners in the firm need to make.

Then and only then will the path to greater Partner contribution open up, and only then will the Coiled Springs see not just that they can become Accelerators, but that they *should* become Accelerators.

It is often by working with the Coiled Springs and stimulating a different contribution from that group that a firm can begin to start thinking of a changed destiny. This is the group to focus on. I believe many in the group would welcome making an input that was wider than just their billing. Who knows what the firm might unleash.

When work with this group starts, one of two things might happen:

1. The Coiled Spring avidly embraces all things "Accelerator" – a great result

2. The Coiled Spring refuses to embrace the new ways and thus potentially starts a journey down the slippery slope to becoming a Roadblock

The Accelerator

This is a high bar to get over. These Partners are moving towards the front of the bus.

Even before any partnership brainstorm of the sort I have just mentioned, you can get Partners who are literally Accelerators in a firm, and maybe even Drivers (though they won't always know exactly where they are heading).

Where there has been a partnership brainstorm, and a set of broad rails has been agreed that the Team Leaders will take out to the team level, an opportunity is created for Coiled Springs to really start contributing to the business as owners and stakeholders. They can become Accelerators.

Accelerators exhibit Leadership Behaviours and they embrace all aspects of The Money Journey and the firm's way. They lead by example and demonstrate to the internal world that the hard and soft rules apply to them, too. That all goes towards building a firm's way. As their name suggests, they help the firm to move forward. Law firms need lots of Accelerators. They are very welcome in any firm. They aid decision-making and are willing to give things a go.

Key features of Accelerators (who can be found across the fee-earning and the Business Support teams in a law firm) include some or all of the following:

- They are self-aware and are keen to learn to be a leader rather than a mere boss

- They are perhaps not in charge of any group (yet), but they still exhibit all Leadership Behaviours

- They don't (yet) instigate Leadership Actions, but they support those that do

- They enable and assist firm and team decisions to be made

- They visibly lend their support to the team's or the firm's leaders, and their decisions

- They accept cabinet responsibility for decisions that are made

- They embrace and strengthen all four legs of the stool

- They treat clients as clients of the whole firm, not as "my client"

- They are happy for the firm to engage with clients without their involvement

- They embrace the rails and try to move everyone along them

- They believe in and embrace the firm's way and its various parts

- They accept that no one is bigger than the firm

The Driver

This is a really high bar to get over. These are the people who make the real difference. A Partner can't make the same difference by, for example, billing a lot. Drivers make a real difference by getting a group of people to row more effectively in a different direction in a sustained, consistent way.

Drivers are committed to strengthening all four legs of the stool, they understand and value all aspects of The Money Journey, and they are keenly involved in designing rails and keeping everyone (i.e., a wide group) on them and moving along them. They live the firm's way. They exhibit all Leadership Behaviours, take Leadership Actions, and lead by example.

You can find Drivers in a number of places in a law firm:

1. Drivers might be found amongst those Partners who are already in a formal leadership or management position in the firm, but where, in that role, they go much further than Accelerators and bring about real, widespread change on the part of a group of people by behaving as effective leaders. A "Team Leader" who has been the "leader" of the team for years, but where the team hasn't materially grown, is not a Driver. They might instead be an Accelerator. They might actually be a Roadblock, where the team might actually have shrunk during their "leadership" of it, and they should long ago have stepped down or been stepped down. Not being a Driver in these positions deprives the team and the firm of a major opportunity for growth

2. As I mentioned, in a law firm you occasionally find what I always think is a really good state of affairs where someone who isn't the most senior person in the team is the Team Leader. To me, that shows great vision, maturity, courage, and

acumen by the firm, and it shows these good qualities to an even greater degree on the part of Partners or Equity Partners in that team who are happy for a "junior" person to be their Team Leader. The reason a "junior" person is Leader of the Team is usually because they have demonstrated clear Driver qualities, which include Leadership Behaviours and Leadership Actions of course. Well done them, well done the firm, and well done the more senior people who have agreed to their elevation.

3. Sometimes, within a main team, you can have a lawyer (possibly a Partner, but they don't need to be) who effectively runs a business within the team but not in a silo or isolated kind of way where contrary attitudes and behaviours prevail. These "superstar" or "potential superstar" lawyers can have a high profile that attracts work of a certain type, or they are responsible for a range of clients or for a particular "sub-work-type", and they run their team in the way that the wider team that they are part of is run (or in an even better way), exhibiting all Leadership Behaviours. I frequently see this and I always advocate that such sub-leaders be brought into the sunlight so that they form a new main team instead of being under the shadow of a larger, broader team and its leader. The results, when you water a leadership plant in this way, can be amazing.

4. As with Accelerators, Drivers aren't only found in the fee-earning side of the business. You can find them in the Business Support team, too,

leading HR, IT, Finance, Learning & Development, etc, teams where they are hell-bent on making a long-lasting difference to the law firm, the organisation, and the business.

That is, a difference that fits in with the firm's leadership's plans, rather than just doing their own thing and doing what they themselves think is best for the business. They are team players. You absolutely need Drivers in all these aspects – what they can achieve leaves behind even a high-billing Partner's contribution.

In my model, those then are the four broad categories that a Partner in a law firm can fall into. I need to make a few related points in relation to these categories, though.

First, within most of these categories, yes, there are shades, but a Roadblock is a Roadblock is a Roadblock. Even at the "good" end of that category, a Partner is still just that – someone who is stopping the progress of the firm and reducing the prospects of everyone in the firm. Whilst they remain a Roadblock (or whilst there is a Roadblock Partner in the firm), the firm cannot have its way of doing things.

Second, there is fluidity and mobility between these Partner categories. Up or down. Everyone loves a sinner who repents, and the Roadblock who improves is to be celebrated. The Coiled Spring who becomes an Accelerator can become a truly compelling influencer, to say nothing of the Accelerator who becomes a Driver. If they can do it, these movers can and should shout, "You can all do it too!" A once-recalcitrant

Partner can become a champion, a beacon, a real motivator of others.

This mobility obviously requires a level of self-awareness and an exercise in honest self-examination, leading to a private or collaborative series of actions to change the Partner's direction and speed of travel.

Third, it is the job of any leader (at any level) to find the next leaders. The Managing Partner needs to be constantly on the lookout for the next leader of the firm, and for the next leaders in the firm. The overall leader of the firm and the person responsible in the firm for the development of its people (the Head of HR, for example) need to have a programme in place that stimulates leadership awareness, thinking, and behaviours at every level in the firm. Anyone can be a leader, and a law firm needs lots of leadership. When a Managing Partner sees someone showing leadership potential, that potential should not be snuffed out by telling the person their billing is poor. Leadership ought to be one of the qualities that enhances rather than hinders reward and progression in a law firm.

Fourth, leadership begets leadership. No one can learn leadership or improve their leadership skills just by reading books, watching webinars, or listening to podcasts. You learn and hone leadership by leading. In a small way, to start with, and by being self-aware, by genuinely working hard to learn and to exhibit Leadership Behaviours and to instigate Leadership Actions, and by asking for feedback. By trying things, by making mistakes, and by thus getting better at helping people to come together as a team and to realise individual and group potential. The firm's current leaders should create leadership opportunities for people all over the firm, and give people who embrace those opportunities the training, the tools, and the space to learn and improve as leaders.

Fifth, in terms of the numbers of each Partner type, it takes lots of effort from Drivers and Accelerators to move and to re-focus a large ship and to overcome inertias that flow from decades of a firm having done things a certain way.

It only takes one Roadblock to spoil everything, for whilst there are Roadblocks in the firm, there can be no group leadership by the Partners and there can be no "way" that the firm can boast of. Rails lose their value and their impact when they don't apply to one or more Partners in a team or a firm.

In short, using the definitions I have used in this chapter, Drivers pressing Accelerators, with the potential in The Coiled Springs being unleashed and harnessed, with no Roadblocks to slow down progress, is the way for Partners, partnerships, and law firms to go.

CHAPTER 23

CONCLUSIONS

As this book completes my law firm "Management" trilogy, please allow me to pull together some conclusions not just in relation to what makes The Perfect Partner but also in relation to the whole shooting match – The Perfect Legal Business, The Perfect Lawyer, and The Perfect Partner – as they so clearly all fit together.

The various themes and concepts that I have discussed in this particular book all come together to enable a firm to shoot for the stars:

- The firm needs Partners made of the right stuff

- Discipline across the firm – in the form of rails – is needed

- They need to be the right rails so that all four legs of the stool are constantly strengthened

- To get to that point, Partners need to make decisions

- Partners also need to exhibit Leadership Behaviours

- Leaders then need to take or support Leadership Actions – to arrive at the rails and to move the firm along them

- The firm needs to enable and reward these contributions at every level

- If all of this happens in a firm, that firm will have *its way* of doing things

If the overall aim is to have a law firm (or rather, a legal business) that brings long-term security, stability, wealth, and health to its clients, its people, and its owners, these are the very clear areas that a law firm should focus on. Noise, low-margin work, high-volume work, top-line growth, "new matter openings" graphs, and rankings based on turnover should not have any priority. These are hard work, high cost, high risk, and are of relatively low value.

Instead, stick to the basics and do less, better, for more. Let the noisy world that is the legal sector go on around you, and become one of those rare law firm beasts – a calm, serene business that is profit-rich, cash-rich, and very happy.

Unless you are a law firm with team Gross Margins exceeding 60% and with no debtors, where profit is rising each year and that profit is in the form of cash, where client service is consistently great across the whole firm, where your clients use all your teams, where your good people stay and more of their ilk are queuing up to come through your front door, then there is room for your business to improve. Identify the rails you need, agree them, and stick to them. Set out what your way is going to be. These should be the headings in your "Strategy" document and in your Partner "awayday" agenda.

As I said in the Introduction to this book, you all know all of this. Making it happen is the hard part. Making it all happen at once is even harder.

But it can and does all happen! I see it all happen and fall into place at the law firms I work with, and quickly, too. What does that tell you? It tells me that these things are indeed perfectly possible and that what is standing in the way is people who are too busy to take stock and then embrace practices to reduce their workloads and, at the same time, generate more money and deliver better service. We need to punch through all of this, and the main punchers and fighters that we need to call upon are the Partners in the firm.

I am now satisfied that the improvements needed – although they are well-known by firms – cannot all come in the required timescale solely as a result of the efforts of the Managing Partner and the Senior Management Team. They usually know what is needed, but them simply issuing orders won't achieve what we need here.

The conclusion I have reached, having been immersed in this exploration for decades, is that we need to turn and look at the Partners in a firm. Cometh the hour, cometh the Partners. And the hour is very much here.

First, Partners need to have an open mind as to whether improvement is possible and needed, rather than having a closed mind. They need an open mind as to what measures should be tried in order to get the improvement that is needed. Burying heads in sand, or believing they absolutely know what is right in a theatre where few Partners have had any real training, or arguing rather than just trying something, is a handbrake on progress.

Next, the things that are needed involve making decisions. We can't go anywhere until a firm lubricates its decision-making processes. Partners can stop any decision being reached. And even once a decision has been made, nothing much can happen without the Partners deciding to do it.

To generate profit and cash at the requisite levels in a sustainable way, the Partners in a law firm need to be at the head of a firm-wide and joined-up crusade to identify the necessary rails and to drive the firm along them, taking all the firm's people with them. A law firm is a million miles away from the Coke seller we looked at earlier in the book. There is a huge array of obstacles to overcome to ensure that (1) the teams and the firm generate enough profit and (2) it's not a "paper" profit, it's actual cash.

But Partners can't do these things bluntly and mechanically. Machines and humans can collide, and the outcome is rarely good. Instead, Partners need to adopt the decent, reasonable traits that I call Leadership Behaviours in this book. There are hard requirements on Partners to do and to promote specific business practices, but the requirements on them if we are to see the rise of the perfect legal business go much deeper than that. A law firm, when all is said and done, is a people business. Flawed but financially productive Partners may help to keep a firm where it is, but they stop it from going further and risk pushing it back.

Some Partners may be born flawed, and others may become flawed because that's what the law firm requires of them, and that's what the firm rewards them for. With the best will in the world, a good Partner will focus solely on their personal billing at the expense of everything else, if that's what their salary or profit share depends on. The firm might thus unwittingly be keeping the Partners as Coiled Springs or even turning them into Roadblocks where they have good billing levels personally but are utterly destructive in terms of lawyer retention, development, productivity, and departures.

There will be a good outcome for the business if each Partner does what is necessary both in billing terms (i.e., in all aspects of The Money Journey) and in Leadership Behaviour terms, but *all* the Partners doing all of these things all of the time will bring a huge, exponential added benefit, namely the secret ingredient called leadership. The Partners not doing so – indeed, *even just one* of them not doing so – has a similarly huge impact, but in the opposite direction.

The aim is to harness the vast energies of all your people combined, and to bring the whole firm together into an unbeatable fighting force.

I use the word "unbeatable" deliberately here. Don't forget, as I said earlier, that the biggest commercial advantage and competitive edge that a law firm has is the fact that all its competitors are, well, law firms. You can therefore guess what is going on in those competitors. There will be a lack of decision-making, meetings where opportunities to improve the business are talked to death, more Partners who are Roadblocks and fewer who are Accelerators and Drivers, a lack of cross-firm leadership by the Partner group, no rails, an absence of focus on the key tools that make up The Money Journey, and no clear *way* of doing things. Let's leave these firms behind!

To look at the size of the opportunity here for Partners to ignite their people and harvest the rewards that follow, can I invite all lawyers reading this to ask themselves two questions:

1. How many Partners changed your life for the better? This question is interesting because you will (I believe) accept without difficulty that a Partner can indeed change your life for the better. It is also interesting because I bet that your answer is that only *one or two* had this great impact across so many Partners with whom you have been involved.

2. How many Partners changed your life for the worse? Again, this is interesting because I expect that we will all readily agree that a Partner does indeed have this terrible power, and because the number here can easily be higher than the number you gave above.

Let's all work together to change the lives of our people, and for the better. Why would you do anything else? How on earth could anything else be for the long-term benefit of the business?

Current law firm Partners might reflect on what people around them in the firm will say about them. Have you changed (or are you currently changing) anyone's life for the better? Or for the worse? What will you be remembered for? Will you be remembered?

And, turning to aspiring Partners, looking ahead to when you become Partners, you might already have formed views as to what kind of Partner you will be. How will your approach then be influenced by what you've seen of Partners up to now?

Good Partner behaviours are contagious, but sadly, so are bad Partner behaviours. Focus on the former and ignore the latter!

I genuinely hope this book has helped you to refine and develop your intentions on the hard business front, but also on the softer people and leadership fronts. I'd say don't keep your powder dry until later – get to work in these areas now and embody the leadership and human principles we have been looking at. If your firm plucks you out of the ranks and propels you forward, you'll know you're in the right place.

A Partner is not another name for a silo. You're in a team. The team is bigger than you. The team will be here long after you've gone. The business needs to invest in its Partners so that during their stewardship, they add to its value and improve its direction and speed and longevity of travel. Let's not take it for granted that anyone "making Partner" will be the leader and businessperson that we need.

How can it be, in light of all that we have looked at in this book, that people within a firm can often become Partners without good and deep training and investment in them so that they add value over and above the value that is inherent in their technical skills?

And really, when you think about it, how can a firm bring in a Partner from outside without ensuring not just that they have the general qualities that a legal business needs, but also that their behaviours are fully and deeply aligned with those of the firm they are joining.

In bringing in a Partner from outside just because they did well in an interview and just because their billing figures look good, or just because you have a gap in a particular team, you might just be bringing in another Roadblock. You can thus get some new billings, but you can lose a whole heap more.

There needs to be a wider and deeper interview process, then an immediate enrolment for everyone at every level into the Academy that I propose, where they are immersed in your way from the outset. And there needs to be a commitment to "getting rid" quickly if the realignment journey doesn't go well.

To close, I hope Partners will see themselves (if they don't already) as but one member of a number of teams. One team is the firm as a whole, and another team is the team that they are actually part of within the firm. The third team that they are a member of, though, is the partnership.

As an organ, a partnership can bring balance, circumspection and wisdom on the one hand. On the other hand, it can bring random, disparate, destructive behaviours if the Partners in the partnership let it, and if the firm – by its reward structure – unwittingly drives Partner behaviours in the wrong direction. Let's leave these dangers to other law firms. Let's recognise the dangers, play to our strengths, and accept that we are small cogs in a big machine that will be here long after we've gone.

If that mentality and that approach is good enough for the greatest sports team that ever walked on this planet, to my mind, it's good enough for a law firm. The All Blacks rugby team have a culture based around a small thing – leaving a changing room better than they found it.

They take the view that however great and famous any or all of them are, all of their number need to have humility, and none of their number is above doing the small things. When they leave a changing room, they all work hard to leave it pristine. Better, in fact, than they found it.

They call it "Sweeping the Shed", and they all do it – even the captain. Their view – and it fits with the terminology we have been using here and the spirit that I hope I have been evoking – is effectively that you can't reach for the stars unless your feet are firmly on the ground.

They believe that better *people* make better All Blacks – not stronger or fitter or faster players. Isn't that exactly what we have seen here?

Better people make better Partners, not bigger billers. Look, for example, at what makes the junior people whom I interviewed for this book go the extra mile, or at what crushes them, and look at how all the Leadership Behaviours I have identified make the world a better place.

Everything we have looked at in assessing what makes The Perfect Partner boils down to this:

- Is your direct contribution to the business of sufficient value (and it needn't be in "billing" terms) to warrant your inclusion in the top team?

- Could you add even more value, though? Do you undermine the value of your direct contribution by failing to act as a team member playing to a team plan, and by failing to be a real leader who is helping to actively lead the wider firm to success?

- Are you keeping the firm where it is, accelerating and driving it forward, or even holding it back?

- Do the Partners and the firm need to come together to facilitate ever-greater things and to free up the power that sits within the partnership?

When it comes to sweeping the shed:

- Would you refuse to, or

- Would you do it if you were asked to, or

- Would you actually *want* to?

And finally, having now completed the Law Firm Management Trilogy, we complete the circle. I hadn't thought of it when I sat down to write the first book, but it is now crystal-clear to me… you cannot have just one or two of The Perfect Lawyer, The Perfect Partner, or The Perfect Legal Business. They are all utterly interlinked and co-dependent.

You need to have all three, or you have none.

Simon McCrum, 2025

Other Books from Simon McCrum

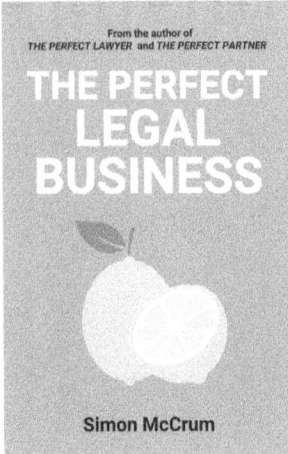

The Perfect Legal Business

What if a law firm's sustained success isn't about billing more and more hours, but shaping its structure, approach, and attitude differently?

In *The Perfect Legal Business*, Simon unlocks a fresh framework for the modern legal firm, built around a number of key pillars including: intelligent client selection, proactive client care, purposeful senior and middle management, higher pricing for a higher level of service, lawyer inputs (not outputs), and the importance of cash to the business – all brought together into a powerful force by the glue that is leadership.

This book invites you to dig deep into law firm management as a constant and fluid problem-solving enterprise – one driven by lawyers at all levels – that seeks to change the fortunes and destinies of law firms, their owners, their people, and their clients.

Note: *The Perfect Legal Business* is the sister book to *The Perfect Lawyer* in that it looks at many of the same themes, but from the viewpoint of the business. As such, it contains material that crosses both titles. If you already have a copy of *The Perfect Lawyer*, you won't need *The Perfect Legal Business*.

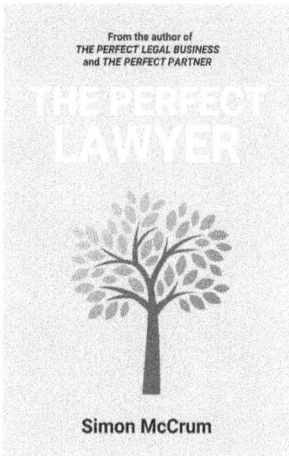

The Perfect Lawyer

What makes a perfect lawyer? To start answering this question, we need to use a classic lawyer approach - it depends!

In *The Perfect Lawyer*, Simon deep dives into what makes a perfect lawyer in a perfect legal business. It is someone who does a great job from the client's perspective but also does a great job from their law firm's – and they are very different things. When combined effectively, such lawyers not only change their clients' lives, but also the destiny of the legal business they work in, and the lives of themselves and their colleagues.

Whether you are part of a large legal firm or a small one, the themes explored in *The Perfect Lawyer* examine the symbiosis between a law firm's team members and the organisation, as they both evolve into higher-earning and more effective entities.

Note: *The Perfect Lawyer* is the sister book to *The Perfect Legal Business* in that it looks at many of the same themes, but from the viewpoint of the individual lawyer. As such, it contains material that crosses both titles. If you already have a copy of *The Perfect Legal Business*, you won't need *The Perfect Lawyer*.

www.ingramcontent.com/pod-product-compliance
Lightning Source LLC
Chambersburg PA
CBHW050450240326
41599CB00064B/7161

*9 7 8 1 9 1 5 8 5 5 4 1 1 *